MOMENTUM

MOMENTUM

Build alignment, action & accountability

Leonie McCarthy

Published by Leonie McCarthy

First published in 2024 in Australia

Copyright© Leonie McCarthy

contact@6r.com.au

This book uses stories to enforce the meaning behind relevant chapters. The business stories and experiences shared in this book are based on real events and interactions. However, to protect the privacy and confidentiality of those involved, some names, identifying details, and scenarios may have been altered, combined, or fictionalised. Any resemblance to specific individuals, companies, or events is purely coincidental. These anecdotes are intended solely for illustrative purposes and to offer insights drawn from professional experience.

Graphics created by Leonie McCarthy

Typeset by BookPOD

Cover design by Brandon McCarthy

ISBN: 978-1-7637619-0-2 (pbk)

ISBN: 978-1-7637619-1-9 (ebook)

A catalogue record for this book is available from the National Library of Australia

Acknowledgements

Every generation reinvents language, creating words that connect them with each other and, often, leave their parents bewildered at best and alienated at worst. It's these quirky phrases that provide humour, insight, and solidarity. A young colleague of mine recently described herself on a long road trip as a "passenger princess." It made me laugh and think deeply about how, in the process of writing this book, I've been something of a passenger princess myself.

My endlessly supportive husband has been my driver on this journey in more ways than one. He's carved out precious time over countless weekends, been a voice of reassurance when I needed it most, and, despite growing weary of the word "change," has wielded his eagle eye for proofreading with tireless patience. I couldn't have done this without his partnership and love.

To all the friends, colleagues, and mentors who have talked this through, read a chapter, or listened to me flounder around with ideas – you have my deepest gratitude. Your time, attention, and insights are priceless gifts, and I hope I've put them to good use. Thank you for being part of this journey with me.

Contents

Introduction

In the modern retail world we're beset by change. This change is often good – it means innovation, growth and new horizons. However, it also puts pressure on the people who need to see the future of their organisation and envision the goals needed to meet that future.

Change projects are one of the best vehicles to use to reach our aspirational goals. They come into being when it's clear that we must improve, rethink or reshape. We start projects because we realise we can't achieve what's required to make the change in the ordinary running of a business. So, the change project, which sits outside our daily business needs, must still be able to fully encompass and serve the future strategy of the business.

That is the challenge.

Some years ago, I worked with a fashion retailer who needed a new enterprise resource program. They chose a top tier system – the best of the best. They seconded people to the project and had multiple consultants supporting them. The project team worked incredibly hard to think through how they would use this ERP system and what it would do for their business.

They did a lot of things right, but the project took longer than they thought – in fact the implementation went on for over 18 months – and as things dragged on it got a bit hairy.

In tandem with the project work, the business was evolving. The business acquired new brands with different types of products (and so different system requirements), it moved into a central corporate office (where it was previously dispersed across multiple locations) and there were new licencing deals in the pipeline. Suffice to say there was 'a bit going on', and pressure to deliver the project was mounting.

I was there in the midst of the chaos, but working on a different project. By pure chance I happened to be in one key meeting where the ERP project team was deciding if they were ready to go live or not. As the COO, who was the project sponsor, went around the room asking team leaders if they were ready, one after another put forward concerns. In every single area there were things that didn't work. And they were all worried.

The team leaders' concerns were each met with the same fate. The COO negotiated, wheedled and offered optimistic views of 'what would be' rather than facing the reality of 'what was', until he'd completely overridden all the concerns. He used his authority to coerce those who reported to him into a 'go' decision. So, they went.

It did not go well.

After they went live they were besieged by problems. The merchandise teams struggled to report on products the way they needed to. Products had only two levels in the new ERP system so it showed the product level, for example, 'shirt', and a descriptive level, for example 'size', but nothing more. This meant that reporting on colour (for example) was next to impossible. Anyone who's worked in fashion knows that black and citron don't behave the same even if they're the same product. What resulted was a flurry of data exports and pivot tables and hours of spreadsheet manipulation that was draining on the time and resources of the employees and the company.

Under the new system as well, previously lax processes were replaced with processes that had hard multi-step dependencies. Receiving inventory became torturous and a backlog in the warehouse developed. Store transfers dried up and individual retail locations were clamouring for stock. It would then arrive in a tidal wave and the tiny stores would be struggling to unpack boxes on the busiest trading days of the week with customers loudly expressing their frustrations.

The training and preparation of teams for the new system was inadequate and those who did know what they were doing were quickly overwhelmed by colleagues who needed help. It got grim. In the mad scramble to Christmas the team rallied on many fronts and managed to get through it (just) but the business suffered – Christmas trade was 25% down on the previous year.

I refer to this as 'implementation via baseball bat' – you get the system in, but there's a hell of a mess to clean up afterwards. Worse, when you don't have the right elements in place, the business itself will suffer – perhaps even fail. And what's the point of making a change if it undermines everything you've already done?

As a project leader, you're responsible for the day-to-day management of change. To meet these needs you need to be able to co-create and contribute to high-performing teams that can collaborate asynchronously and deliver the brief of the client effectively and at speed. In other words, we need to have high performing teams that are uniquely tuned into the process of change.

But building teams that can perform the needed tasks at the needed speed and with the needed proficiency is not easy. It takes considerable and consistent effort to build high-performing teams, and, once achieved, trying to maintain that forward momentum becomes an equal challenge.

Here's a different example project. This business had chosen their provider and were preparing for an implementation that was six months away. Then an opportunity came up. They could take a slot that someone else had dropped out of and do an 'express' implementation.

In twelve weeks.

Yup, half the time that the vendor normally allowed.

This territory is not for everyone, there were some circumstances that made this business consider the express version.

They didn't have many bespoke processes in their existing systems. They didn't have a lot of hard and fast business rules. They didn't have a lot of long tenured staff members who were wedded to the current ways of working.

They did have big expansion plans that would be a lot easier with the new system and a nimble team who were prepared to put in the extra effort that this would be for the long-term gain. They also had sponsors who were prepared to support the team. They were prepared to take the 'default' version of how the software was configured and then work to improve processes post go live.

The sponsors put it to the team. They made the choice together to push for the twelve week express implementation. Everyone understood the purpose. Everyone was aligned in their focus. And everyone was ready to take the action needed.

Short version? They got there.

It was scrappy, and yes there were dramas. Data that was not thoroughly cleansed on migration, products that got mixed up and duplications with barcodes. What really stood out, however, was the way the team worked together to solve the problems that emerged. They worked closely with the vendor to ensure that these issues were sorted out in the immediate post live period – and didn't let them fester.

Contrasting this with the eighteen month baseball bat project scenario, they were able to move inventory on day one, there was minimal impact on customers and store and project teams had the support they needed to work on inevitable problems which they were prepared for.

They still had a mess to clean up post live, but the pain was over faster and they bounced back quickly which set them up well for their growth plans. They achieved what they set out to do – to make a change that embraced their future.

This book is for you

This book will help you if you've got a big change project ahead of you and are looking for some insight into how to achieve successful outcomes and build a high performing team. This book is not a 'how to' guide from beginning to end on project implementation. If you're looking for a how to guide I would suggest starting with *Managing Change in Organizations: A Practice Guide* by Project Management Institute and go from there.

This *is* a book of practical examples – including stories and experiences, research and global context – that can help you build your confidence in the parts of the change project that you have control over.

It *is* a coaching book – designed for the leader who is open to suggestions, experimental enough to try a new way of thinking and innovative enough to know to adjust and adapt these experiences and insights for their own unique business and industry.

It *is* a book that focuses on ensuring that teams are well equipped with an understanding of what they're doing and why and how they can contribute.

It *is* for the leader that recognises that projects start out exciting, but to deliver large ones takes a coordinated effort. Lots of things must go well and there is no magic formula to apply that works across all businesses. Some of those things are in your control as a leader and change manager, and some are not. But by controlling what you can, you are on your way to the outcomes you need.

My hope is that through the pages of this book, we'll get there together.

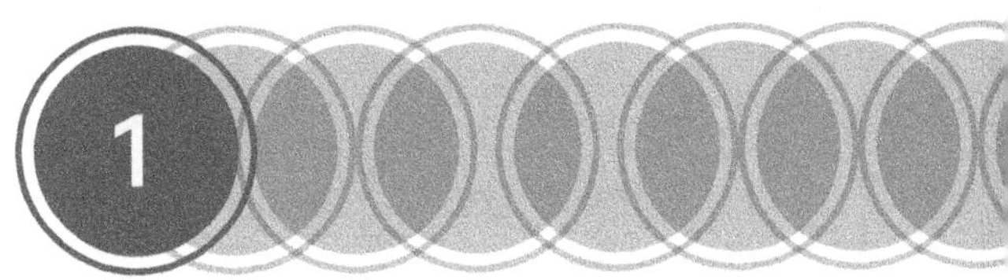

Projects exist within a context

Projects – like anything – exist in a context. This context is your business, your team and your market, of course. But it also encompasses your country, your region and even the world (should we be so bold). This context has a significant influence on how your project will function and whether success is achieved.

If we zoom out to the macro level, the broader economic context and timing in which the project exists influence whether a project is even brought forward as an idea. Political stability and policy environment will also give some context to project work. Whether the project is coming to life in a volatile or stable context will set the mood, tone and even the pace and process for the change project.

The expansion of Tesco's Fresh & Easy into the US market is a notable example of a transformational change project attempted during a difficult economic context. The venture began in 2007, just before the 2008 financial crisis, and ended in 2013 with Tesco's exit from the US market after investing over £1.5 billion in the failed expansion.

The failure of this change effort wasn't solely down to the macro environment. There were plenty of other mis-steps, in supply chain, store format, purchasing preferences and portion sizing that have all been cited as contributing factors to the failure. But because the attempt coincided with the subprime crisis and subsequent economic downturn, particularly impacting consumer spending habits in cities like Las Vegas and Phoenix where Fresh & Easy focused, it was the biggest contributor to its ultimate failure.[12]

The Fresh & Easy project serves as a cautionary tale about the challenges of international expansion without a deep understanding of local culture, consumer preferences and market dynamics. It highlights the importance of thorough research, adaptability and the need to align business models with local consumer behaviours, especially when attempting change in challenging economic times.

So what is the context that we face today as retail organisations looking to implement a change in our own teams and organisations? What about closer to home in Australia and New Zealand? And what about globally?

Context on a team and organisational level

The internal capability of your team(s) and how much of the collective intelligence of your organisation can be directed towards your change project will greatly influence the execution of your project. This is your micro context.

---

1   Butler, S. (9 December 2012). 'Fresh, but not so easy: Tesco joins a long list of British failure in America.' *The Guardian*. https://www.theguardian.com/business/2012/dec/09/fresh-not-easy-tesco-british-failure-america.

2   (12 September 2022). 'International Expansion: Why Tesco Missed the Mark in the U.S. Market.' *Castus*. https://www.castusglobal.com/insights/international-expansion-why-tesco-missed-the-mark-in-the-u-s-market.

A project ecosystem really starts with sponsorship. Sponsorship plays a crucial role in establishing a successful project ecosystem. The right sponsor provides the necessary financial backing and strategic alignment, support, guidance and resources to ensure effective execution throughout the whole life cycle of the project. Sponsors promote the vision or purpose of the project, and have often, through their network or insight, seen a need to make a change in the business. Who the project sponsors are and how they position the project and keep the momentum alive in a business is a significant contributor to success. Sponsors who tire easily or who are too thinly stretched will find it difficult to successfully lead change.

Likewise, project managers who have too many projects competing for their attention will also struggle to make a meaningful difference. While the number of projects managed concurrently by project managers can vary widely, a manageable workload will depend on the project's size and complexity.[3] The project manager who is working across eight different projects (with different clients for each one) will struggle to deliver quality more than a project manager who has 10 smaller projects and is working with a consistent group of similar stakeholders.

The people and resources of the project are temporary. They're borrowed, and they're oftentimes balancing 'business as usual' effort with the additional efforts needed to contribute well to the project. For the change project to be successful, it genuinely needs people who are close to the business context to contribute. These people must be active in the decision-making processes. It is them and their colleagues who will inherit the results of the project.

---

3   Harrin, E. (3 May 2022). 'Help! I'm managing multiple projects.' Association for Project Management. https://www.apm.org.uk/blog/help-i-m-managing-multiple-projects/.

Your project needs technical knowledge. Depending on your organisation this may be within your business. Those who are solution architects or have technical knowledge of existing systems, support the current applications and manage the day-to-day work. For a software project, this should also include your vendor partners and their technical experts who can guide and recommend configuration or implementation methods. Throughout an implementation these people who are working alongside you will also be working to build your expertise in their system.

When it comes to the context of implementing change at a team and organisational level there will be many elements that will impact your project. These are things that will likely be front of mind because they're the things that you'll be seeing in your day-to-day work. You will be faced with a group of individuals from which to draw your project team – and determining the right person for the right role will be the first hurdle – and is one that is absolutely unique to your team, your team members and your project itself.

Amongst other pressures will also be the need to turn your team into change champions. This involves driving buy-in of course, but also creating and maintaining the energy to move the change forward. This is a constant push and pull as things rise up within the context of the project that may impact the individuals themselves and potentially undermine their commitment to the change.

Research shows that 'one of the most critical failures to change' is your team's attitude towards that change, and much of this comes down to a phenomenon known as RTC, or 'resistance to change'.[4] People in general are resistant to change, but in the workplace, this can be energised, becoming bigger than Ben Hur, supported by a sense of fear around their ability to support themselves and their family and by a subconscious sense that the change is unfair. Because of that they may be negative toward the change, exhibiting 'adverse reactions' and making the implementation of any change project more challenging.[5] It therefore becomes hugely important to the success of any change project to begin shaping your team's attitudes towards change, helping them overcome subconscious RTC by making them in effect ready for the change.

However, this isn't a done-in-one effort. The metaphor might be overdone, but managing your team throughout the change process is like herding cats. Each individual is a sinuous, savvy animal, that can easily escape any efforts to bring them into a line. In a group context, this is amplified. Your team – like a herd of cats – is not easily containable or trainable, and there's a lack of predictability in how the project will change and grow, what challenges it will present once it's underway, and, in the same way, there's a lack of predictability in how your team will react. If you pull on a single thread you might find the entire project unravelling.

To counteract these challenges you must also be reviewing and refining during the implementation so that you are getting your team through the change process in the best possible way you can. This is the vital element of care and compassion. And the 'how' of doing that

4   Rehman, N., Mahmood, N. et al. (2021). 'The Psychology of Resistance to Change: The Antidotal Effect of Organizational Justice, Support and Leader-Member Exchange.' *Frontiers in Psychology.* https://www.frontiersin.org/journals/psychology/articles/10.3389/fpsyg.2021.678952/full.

5   Rehman. The Psychology of Resistance to Change.

comes down to alignment, strategy, transparency, communication and accountability (all of which we'll be discussing in the coming chapters!).

Context on the local stage (AU and NZ)

At the start of 2024 the Australian Retail Association (ARA) estimated that Australians spent $24 billion on Boxing Day Sales at the end of 2023.[6] Whilst this represents an increase of 1.6% on the previous year, it doesn't actually mean more money being spent. Higher inflation has had an impact on daily living expenses. So, 'when accounting for population increase and inflation, real retail sales would have fallen by about 6% over that period'.[7]

The ARA is also keen to point out the disparity in what looks like, on the surface, solid sales results. They remind us that household savings rates are near zero and that per capita consumption will likely not increase in 2024 making it a tough year for those relying on discretionary spending.[8] It echoes the predictions of the Economist Intelligence Unit (EIU) report closer to home.

They also cite the difference between larger more established retailers and the smaller and more discretionary ones. While people may continue spending their money in large supermarkets, they may not be frequenting boutiques or gourmet fruit and veg shops, which many view as more expensive generally. So when you're planning a change project

---

6   Side note that anecdotally 'Cyber month' November is gaining on the older school Boxing Day sales.

7   ARA Retail Insights Report 2024. Australian Retailers Association. https://www.retail.org.au/retail-insights-report-2024; Sibal, R. (20 January 202). 'What do shoppers want in a post pandemic world?' Australian Retailers Association. https://www.retail.org.au/news-and-insights/what-do-shoppers-want-in-a-post-pandemic-world.

8   ARA Retail Insights Report 2024; Sibal. What do shoppers want in a post pandemic world?

both the actual increase in spending and what this means in terms of 'real' money need to be considered.

Shifting search & pivoting positioning

To meet the future consumer where they are, retailers need to consider not just their technology and working process but also how their own consumption and carbon footprint is tracked. Retailers that create transparency in their supply chains, create secondary markets and other ways of reusing or recycling products post first purchase, and those who make use of or reuse existing spaces will become the success stories of tomorrow.

We also need to consider how people are finding their local information. Over the last Christmas and New Year period we took a quick drive up the coast to meet some younger cousins for a meal. After dinner, we walked the streets where they were staying (a beachside place) and explored. Chatting with them about eating out and how to find good places, I said something about Google ratings and reviews.

They said, 'No, not Google. Don't even bother. Just look at TikTok.' They showed me.

Together we scrolled for local eateries. TikTok videos of every place that we had just walked past in the main drag appeared. I could see the allure and ease of this platform.[9] Suddenly it felt clunky and old fashioned to have to click through all those Google reviews instead of simply viewing this easy stream of information.[10]

---

9   Galloway, S & Swisher, K. (Hosts). (24 August 2020). Pivot schooled #1: Media's Overnight Chaos, with TikTok's Vanessa Pappas and Columbia University's Emily Bell (Episode 131) [Audio podcast episode]. *Pivot.* https://podcasts. apple.com/ie/podcast/pivot-schooled-1-medias-overnight-chaos-with-tiktoks/ id1073226719?i=1000488968263.

10   Since this experience I have used Google search less and less.

This was an interesting experience (and one that highlighted that I wasn't quite as cool as I once was!). But what really stood out to me is that as a generation, younger people buy very differently. That doesn't just mean the device that they're shopping on[11] (though this matters as well). Trend analysis suggests that Gen Z may be the first generation to have less than their parents had.[12] Take, for example, home ownership, which feels and may be well out of their reach.

But while they may not have more they will certainly know more. They are the most well educated generation to date, particularly women.[13] They have access to more information about the world than any generation before them. They've grown up connected to it, attuned to their place in it and how to make their mark on it. To me, they seem attracted to self-expression, flocking to stores and sites that allow for the creation of the exact personal shade of lipstick, the perfect fragrance for the pending nuptials or the right tattoo art for the earscape. They also have strong desires to shop second hand and give pre-owned products a new life.[14]

I'm observing the rise of B corporations and greater demand for supply chain transparency, data privacy and management. The rise of plugins showing resale price estimates for your new designer handbag speak

---

11 Gen Z (42 percent) and millennial (46 percent) consumers are far more likely to make purchases on their mobile phones at least monthly compared to Gen X (29 percent) and baby boomers (13 percent). Keenan, J. (8 September 2020). 'Report: Omnichannel Experiences Must Extend to Gift Cards.' TotalRetail. https://www.mytotalretail.com/article/omnichannel-experiences-must-extend-to-gift-card-purchasing/.

12 Dickler, J. (27 January 2024). 'In many ways, Gen Zers are better off than their parents were 30 years ago, but fewer are financially independent – here's why.' CNBC. https://www.cnbc.com/2024/01/27/gen-z-vs-their-parents-how-the-generations-stack-up-financially.html.

13 Dickler. In many ways, Gen Zers are better off than their parents were 30 years ago, but fewer are financially independent – here's why.

14 '40% of Gen Z turn to resale to find the styles they're looking for.' WGSN. https://www.wgsn.com/en/blogs/40-gen-z-turn-resale-find-styles-theyre-looking#:~:text=Gen%20Z%20consumers%20are%20accelerating,with%20an%20alternative%20income%20stream.

to an awareness of a life after purchase. Whether this is just a salving of conscience will remain to be seen. Or maybe this is a genuine effort to give preloved items another life before the inevitable landfill.[15] In Europe, the right to repair legislation will come in shortly. While we are yet to see these impacts closer to home, we are seeing more repair options being offered at high end or highly conscious brands[16]. Changes to packaging laws and clearly labelling allergens on food packaging may also lead us to improved transparency through (at least) the food supply chain.

Supply chain strategy

In Australia and New Zealand, we are heavily dependent on international shipping. The distance and time that it takes to get here are not lost on tourists or traders. Importing or exporting goods presents unique challenges for businesses operating in Australia. Most retail businesses have some level of exposure, either directly or indirectly simply because it takes a long time for people and things to get here. Even within our country, from the eastern seaboard to Western Australia (WA), the time and cost to transport goods is a significant cost line to manage.

In Australia, transport is mostly by road, and accessibility can vary significantly in more remote parts of the country, making transport and logistics of particular importance for local retailers. When train lines are damaged (which will happen more frequently as we see changes in weather patterns), it's difficult to get goods to WA. Business leaders are left with choices that are uncomfortable and a punt no matter what they choose. Take a chance on road transport and pay significantly higher costs for delivery? Or use sea freight and add time and effort to the

---

15 '2024 Event Recap: Back to the Big Apple.' NRF.com. https://nrfbigshow.nrf.com/about/2024-event-recap.

16 Zarha, P. [Host]. (23 August 2024). Building brands with purpose with Joanne Mercer. [Audio podcast episode]. In Retail Therapy. Australian Retailers Association. https://retailtherapy.podbean.com/e/building-brands-with-purpose-with-joanne-mercer/.

rerouting of goods? Or wait for the train lines to be repaired and risk empty shelves? Whichever you choose is a roll of the dice.

Supply chain strategies are an important part of every retailer's growth strategy, yet it's one that requires flexibility and agility in order to embrace well. The supply chains that refresh, relist and redistribute goods that have already been sold once new, and now can achieve a second and third (and further!) life will gain importance in the economic landscape of tomorrow. But all this points to greater fragmentation in the retail industry. Retailers need to focus on personalising their marketing in order to gain a competitive advantage and get the most value out of the dollars they're spending per customer acquisition. It's a challenge but it's also an opportunity.

Repurposed products

Now and in the immediate and long-term future it's likely that younger consumers will push for ethical supply chains and better transparency as a much more important part of their decision-making equation. The list of retailers working toward B Corp status on my feed and the increasing availability of market like sites that offer connections to brands that are more transparent in their social agendas is growing. And the newer generations are fully on board.

It's also likely we'll see a deeper focus on the post-purchase life of products. The introduction or some evolution of the right to repair that is gaining ground elsewhere should also be seen on our shores. Couple this with the rise of Gen Z and Gen Alpha and their approach to repurposing products and the shift on how and what we consume will, in the coming years, be significant.

Making a pit stop in a country town on the way home from a trip to the Southern Highlands recently, I popped into the local Vinnies, which was pumping on a Sunday morning. People of all ages and types were browsing the shelves open to the opportunity that someone else's donation is a worthwhile purchase that will find another life and use pre landfill.[17] Another indication of what's important to consumers today.

There are those who talk about renewable retail. I'm not sure how renewable retail really is as an industry. Shopping centres that are abandoned are not easily repurposed. Products not sold are dumped in landfill, from garments to bikes and electronics.

'Where have all the Cabbage Patch Kids gone?' asks Hannah Gadsby, whose stand up comedy show is a funny but poignant questioning of what we should be worrying about in the 'sea of contemporary anxieties, problems and disasters.'[18] It's a valid question. If you can remember the mania and importance of Cabbage Patch Kids, then you will appreciate how many of them must be suffocating in a pile of garbage somewhere.

Unfortunately, the recycling industry in Australia is broken.[19] We've got good intentions but awful execution. We have convinced ourselves that putting cardboard and bottles in recycling bins is enough and that somewhere behind the curtain our hastily assembled discarded packaging is being put to better use. It is not.

Much of our recycling efforts are focused on short-term solutions. Countries like Germany and South Korea are showing that it's possible to make this work without adding too much additional cost to the consumer. Peter Börkey, of the OECD Environment Directorate, suggests

17 I was lucky to find the perfect shade of bath mat to match my new bathroom in this op shop.

18 Tongue, C. (10 March 2024). 'Woof! review – Hannah Gadsby refuses to toe the line.' *The Guardian*. https://www.theguardian.com/australia-news/2024/mar/10/woof-review-hannah-gadsby-refuses-to-toe-the-line.

19 (2 March 2023). 'Australia's recycling crisis.' The Squiz. https://www.thesquiz.com.au/shortcuts/australias-recycling-crisis/.

we 'encourage the development of extended producer responsibility systems, ideally harmonised across states and with some guidance provided by the Commonwealth.'[20] I'm on board, but my pandemic lessons from watching the state Premiers attempt to cooperate have not left me with much hope for this delightfully well-coordinated approach.

So maybe as consumers we'll get better at reusing or resharing our 'one time only' needed products. Maybe we'll pass them on and reduce the need for new ones. Logic says that the overall demand for traditional product-based businesses will decrease. But then the inevitable question for those of us operating in the retail space arises. If the use we get from products improves and extends how do retailers remain in business, stay profitable and continue to grow?

It's not going to be possible for everyone to have all the 'stuff' that we've been convinced we need. The basic math doesn't even work. 72% of our population lives in cities, and yet everyone wants to have a big backyard, be close to work and school and not have to spend hours each day commuting from A to B. Only a very small amount of the continent of Australia is hospitable to modern living, yet we have a generous mindset when it comes to personal space.

Hope for the future

Despite the waste and chaos, there are actions where I see hope. Recently my son bought himself a new keyboard. He spent a good deal of time and energy researching which keyboard to purchase so that it can be repaired. In his case, each individual key can be replaced if needed. We have long discussed this idea around the dinner table and how difficult it is that computers are not more repairable. It's so

---

20   Baker, N & Quince, A. (14 June 2023). 'How can Australia improve its household waste and recycling systems?' *ABC.* https://www.abc.net.au/news/2023-06-14/how-can-australia-improve-its-household-waste-and-recycling-syst/102451122.

frustrating for something to be microseconds 'out of warranty' and have the manufacturer be completely uninterested in fixing it. The alternative is that the maker will repair it, but it will cost the same as purchasing a new one.

My aunt, mid-COVID, was irritated at the idea that she couldn't get anyone to fix her vacuum cleaner. 'Get a new one,' said my uncle, but instead she took herself off to spare parts places to find the bolt that would solve her problem. The parts place didn't even charge her for the bolt, and she had the enormous satisfaction of fixing the broken vacuum herself – a new one was not required! The problem for the manufacturer is the missed opportunity of having an ongoing relationship with their customer, not just missing being able to charge for the bolt, the service or a replacement unit, but to cement the relationship with the customer so that they feel connected to the brand and potentially recommend to others or they themselves buy again.

It's interesting that the shift for new generations of consumers suggests a trend towards services and experiences. The theatre of retail space, the third space – a place to meet, see and be seen – is still alive and well. People still want to be out doing, connecting and meeting. There are possibilities to explore that include aftermarket services and repair, experiences and education about the product. Among all this shifting push and pull back and forth through the value chain, the focus on trying to satisfy and occasionally delight an increasingly cynical and well-educated consumer, is the mandate to create something new, interesting, engaging and exciting that customers will want to hand over their cash for.

> The theatre of retail space, the third space – a place to meet, see and be seen – is still alive and well.

Of the external pressures that retailers are operating under here in Australia, the ones that we really need to consider when undertaking any change project look to our future. It seems deeply obvious that if we consume more than we produce, we will eventually run out of resources. It's a bit like eating nothing but junk food and hoping that we will somehow lose weight. The basic mathematics of the situation just don't work. Eventually our rate of consumption must slow.

The idea that buying one good quality item, and repairing it multiple times, possibly even handing it on to someone else to use, is a more peaceful and sustainable way to live. As retailers this is what we know must happen – yet our fixation on constant growth without understanding the greater context can hurt us.

Context on the global stage

Innovation at risk

Fareed Zakaria, a writer and geopolitical observer, has asked, 'Are we living through the most revolutionary period in history?'[21] Well, we might be. Fareed has spent 10 years researching and writing his most recent book, *Age of Revolutions: Progress and Backlash from 1600 to the Present,* which traces historical arcs from the 1600s through today by looking at modern politics.[22] In his book, Zakaria talks about how he believes that left and right in politics are no longer relevant. Instead, we are seeing the rise of more open or closed philosophies. Open countries

---

21 Dubner, S. [Host]. (3 April 2024). Are We Living Through the Most Revolutionary Period in History? (No. 583) [Audio podcast episode.] In Freakonomics Radio. https://freakonomics.com/podcast/are-we-living-through-the-most-revolutionary-period-in-history/.

22 Zakaria, F. (2024). *Age of Revolutions: Progress and Backlash from 1600 to the Present.* W. W. Norton & Company.

and cultures embrace more inclusive politics, technology, and diversity, while closed countries and cultures are more protectionist.[23]

In 2024 the annual Edelman Trust Barometer[24] documented that 24 of the 28 countries surveyed were at all-time lows when it came to institutional trust. The trust measure dropped sharply by 10 points year on year from 2022, with only a mild wavering through the pandemic years. The report has captured the current mood: 'Innovation in Peril' is the headline for 2024.

This shift away from political and technological openness and the reduction of trust in institutions, puts innovation – including on the retail stage – on uncertain footing. Without the global community's support of organisations to implement change and innovation, the context becomes more and more challenging. We will struggle to shape our future culture as we hurtle without a seatbelt towards the, some say inevitable, brick wall ahead.

Politics and the polarisation paradox

Polarisation and paradox could well be the underlying themes of the moment. What does that mean? Well, within our world we're becoming both more split in outlook – moving further and further along the spectrum (the polarisation) and more insulated in our thinking (the paradox).

The amount of information we're exposed to, or have access to if sought out, has increased exponentially. To illustrate this, approximately 402.74 million terabytes of data are created each day. This has increased around

---

23   Zakaria. Age of Revolutions.
24   Edelman Trust Barometer (2024). Global Report. Online Fieldwork in 28 Countries. https://www.edelman.com/trust/2024/trust-barometer.

74x from just two zettabytes in 2010. And it's expected to increase by over 150% to 181 zettabytes by 2025.

To put that into perspective, experts estimate that 90% of the world's data was generated in the last two years alone.[25] But despite living in a world where huge amounts of information and diverse opinions are easily accessible, we're in fact becoming less and less exposed to everything that's out there. Our echo chambers are deepening, and this is adding to both the polarisation and the insulation.

It takes only a few moments on any media forum to see that politics are becoming more extreme and our tolerance of differing opinions less common. We have unwittingly embraced algorithms that create (social) media bubbles (aka echo chambers) that 'echo' our own opinions back to us over and over. These make us feel that we are among the majority of thinkers on a topic despite a much broader world of thinking and opinions existing.

This, coupled with our diminishing attention span (in 2004, people averaged 150 seconds on any screen before switching to another screen; by 2012, it declined to 75 seconds; by 2021, it fell to 47 seconds[26]), has made us unused to sitting across from those with different opinions and less willing to consider things from others' points of view. So while we have access to more information than ever, we're instead hunkering down into our own insulated viewpoints.

I've observed since the pandemic that we see more and more physical markers that indicate a lack of tolerance. Signs at check in counters reminding me as a customer that I need to be polite or that I'm on

---

25   Taylor, P. (16 November 2023). Volume of data/information created, captured, copied, and consumed worldwide from 2010 to 2020, with forecasts from 2021 to 2025. Statista. https://www.statista.com/statistics/871513/worldwide-data-created/.

26   Mark, G. (2023). *Attention Span: A Groundbreaking Way to Restore Balance, Happiness and Productivity.* Hanover Square Press.

camera. IVR (Interactive Voice Response) systems that attempt to curtail waiting customers' frustrations by reminding them that abuse is not tolerated. There are studies and statistics that support it too. These studies show that those who work in retail are subjected to more and more verbal abuse from customers who are trying to get their own way or game a system. In 2023, a survey of more than 4,600 retail workers reported that 87% of those workers had experienced some form of verbal abuse from a customer, and 12.5% reported physical violence. In that same survey, 52% reported that they'd had the same customer act abusive or violent on more than one occasion.[27]

When things are uncertain, most people get stressed. Uncertainty triggers stress by activating the amygdala, the brain's fear center, which initiates the 'fight-or-flight' response, releasing stress hormones like cortisol and adrenaline.[28] This leads to physiological changes such as increased heart rate, rapid breathing and muscle tension. Additionally, uncertainty can cause elevated levels of dopamine, which stimulates the sympathetic nervous system, causing heightened alertness and anxiety.[29]

The pandemic hasn't helped. Post-pandemic, we've been left with a residual heightened level of stress and anxiety among the general public, which leads to increasing frustration, shorter fuses and aggressive behaviour in everyday interactions, including in retail settings. So what

---

27 Minister for Industrial Relations & Minister for Work Health and Safety. (27 March 2024). 'Shoppers urged to show respect to retail workers ahead of Easter rush.' [Press release]. https://www.nsw.gov.au/media-releases/shoppers-urged-to-show-respect-to-retail-workers-ahead-of-easter-rush.

28 Lewis, M. (5 April 2016). 'Why we're hardwired to hate uncertainty.' *The Guardian*. https://www.theguardian.com/commentisfree/2016/apr/04/uncertainty-stressful-research-neuroscience.

29 LeWine, H. E. [Reviewer]. (3 April 2024). ' Understanding the stress response: Chronic activation of this survival mechanism impairs health.' *Harvard Health Publishing*. https://www.health.harvard.edu/staying-healthy/understanding-the-stress-response.

we're seeing in retail is just an experience that is more or less universal to the human experience post pandemic. We've had high levels of danger and uncertainty[30] followed by economic tightening.[31]

This has meant that retail, where people are often short of time or under some sort of financial pressure, can become a kind of hotspot where tensions manifest. Whilst industry body representatives call out for governments[32] to do more or do better, we also must take some personal responsibility for our own behaviour.

An eye for economics

Economic factors are a huge part of driving and shaping organisational change. There is an undeniable interplay between the economy and organisational evolution. When it comes to implementing a change project, you need to understand the global economic forces at play and have given some thought to what (if anything) might impact your change.

Today, economic conditions are tightening globally. The long period of unprecedented near zero interest rates ended in 2022. This is despite a belief at the time that, at least in the US, eurozone and the UK, they would stay stable at extremely low rates for the foreseeable future. By October

---

30 Let's not forget the 2019 bushfires that ravaged much of Australia's eastern states.

31 Ferrante, F et al. (January 2024). 'The international spillovers of synchronous monetary tightening.' *Journal of Monetary Economics*. https://www.sciencedirect.com/science/article/abs/pii/S0304393223001320.

32 (10 November 2023). 'Employers and employees join forces to address rising customer violence in retail.' [Media release]. Australian Retailers Association. https://www.retail.org.au/media/employers-and-employees-join-forces-to-address-rising-customer-violence-in-retail; 'The key issues: Customer abuse & aggression toward retail workers.' Essential Retail. https://essentialretail.com.au/the-issues/customerabuse/.

2022, the mood had shifted, and previous optimism was replaced with the widespread expectation that recession was imminent.[33]

From 2023 many countries around the world have begun to experience inflation.[34] While currently inflation is predicted to steady and in some countries decline, most global households and organisations are operating in an economy that has shrunk and may remain that way for some time.[35]

Of course, things can and likely will change by 2025.[36] And as an ever fluctuating element, you must consider the state of the global economy, and its impact on your organisation, particularly supply partners and currency risks when embarking on change projects.

Technology (traps)

Today manipulation of mainstream media is something we now, if not accept, are at least alive to the existence of.[37]

---

33 Frankel, J. (13 August 2023). 'The End of Zero Interest Rates.' Harvard Kennedy School Belfer Center for Science and International Affairs. https://www.belfercenter. org/publication/end-zero-interest-rates

34 Shipman, A et al. (5 January 2023). 'Global economy 2023: how countries around the world are tackling the cost of living crisis.' *The Conversation*. https:// theconversation.com/global-economy-2023-how-countries-around-the-world-are-tackling-the-cost-of-living-crisis-196740.

35 World Economic Outlook, April 2024; Steady but Slow: Resilience amid Divergence; April 16, 2024 https://www.imf.org/en/Publications/WEO/Issues/2024/04/16/world-economic-outlook-april-2024

36 (2 May 2024). 'Economic outlook: Steady global growth expected for 2024 and 2025.' [Press release]. Organisation for Economic Co-operation and Development. https://www.oecd.org/en/about/news/press-releases/2024/05/economic-outlook-steady-global-growth-expected-for-2024-and-2025.html#:~:text=The%20 global%20economy%20is%20continuing,up%20to%203.2%25%20in%202025..

37 Hern, A. (20 June 2017). 'Facebook and Twitter are being used to manipulate public opinion – report. *The Guardian*. https://www.theguardian.com/ technology/2017/jun/19/social-media-proganda-manipulating-public-opinion-bots-accounts-facebook-twitter; Stent, D. (31 August 2018). 'Social Media Manipulation of Public Opinion in Korean Elections.' *The Diplomat*. https://thediplomat. com/2018/09/social-media-manipulation-of-public-opinion-in-korean-elections/.

One of the more alarming moments goes back to the Cambridge Analytica scandal. The fallout saw the company facing multiple investigations and legal challenges. In terms of accountability, the focus was primarily on Facebook and its leadership for failing to protect user data.[38] In 2022 Meta (the parent company of Facebook) settled out of court. $725 million sounds like a lot until you deduct legal and administrative costs and look at the sheer number of complainants in the case. Some estimates have calculated that each claimant who submitted a valid claim will likely only receive only about $30.[39]

The breakneck speed of artificial intelligence (AI) experimentation and the swift adoption of generative AI has driven a significant shift since its release in 2023.

Sadly, the pace of legislation and regulation is not keeping up with the creative ways to exploit human fallibility. We struggle in the moment to stop, examine our own fears and failings and question the motivation of some of the content that we consume. It's too easy to allow ourselves to be influenced by the scroll.

The breakneck speed of artificial intelligence (AI) experimentation and the swift adoption of generative AI has driven a significant shift since its release in 2023. But is this a good thing? In 2020 OpenAI published a press release saying that GPT2

---

38 McCallum, S. (23 December 2022). 'Meta settles Cambridge Analytica scandal case for $725m.' *BBC News*. https://www.bbc.com/news/technology-64075067.

39 Martichoux, A. (9 August 2023). 'How big will Facebook settlement checks be? Lawyers reveal estimated payment per person.' *The Hill*. https://thehill.com/homenews/nexstar_media_wire/4193231-how-big-will-facebook-settlement-checks-be-lawyers-reveal-estimated-payment-per-person/.

(forerunner of ChatGPT) was a tool 'too dangerous' to release to the public and that it represented 'security and safety concerns'.[40] Further experts believe that this type of AI could be easily used for 'malicious purposes', such as spreading fake news and information.[41]

We've seen this happen with devastating consequences. Recently a Reddit user posted asking for advice when their entire family was poisoned after using an AI-generated book on mushroom foraging sold by a 'major online retailer'.[42] The user claimed that there was no indication that the book was AI generated, but after they were hospitalised, they took a closer look and realised that even the images of the mushrooms themselves were AI generated.

There is a concern as well that AI could become so powerful that it could replace professional experts in most industries within the next decade. In fact a 2023 report by Goldman Sachs suggested that artificial intelligence (AI) could replace a staggering 300 million full time jobs, reducing employment opportunities and wage levels in the short term.[43]

Still, it was released.

Not only was it released to a public scrambling to keep up, but those developing ChatGPT have consumed almost 200,000 books **without**

40   Webb, A. (30 March 2023). 'Amy Webb Launches 2023 Emerging Tech Trend Report [Conference presentation].' SXSW 2023, Austin, Texas, United States. https://www.youtube.com/watch?v=vMUpzxZB3-Y.

41   Vincent, J. (7 November 2019). 'OpenAI has published the text-generating AI it said was too dangerous to share.' The Verge. https://www.theverge.com/2019/11/7/20953040/openai-text-generation-ai-gpt-2-full-model-release-1-5b-parameters.

42   [Virtual_Cellist_736] (16 August 2024). Family poisoned after using AI-generated mushroom identification book we bought from major online retailer. [Online forum post]. Reddit. https://www.reddit.com/r/LegalAdviceUK/comments/1etko9h/family_poisoned_after_using_aigenerated_mushroom/.

43   Vallance, C. (29 March 2023). 'AI could replace equivalent of 300 million jobs - report.' BBC. https://www.bbc.com/news/technology-65102150.

consent.[44] This has focused attention on the theft of work that has taken decades for humans to create. Authors have expressed dismay, anger and outrage.

One author, Mary H. K. Choi said, 'I'm furious and want to fight but I'm also so tired.' She explained herself further: 'A book encapsulates infinite choices, boundless permutations and even shortcomings of the author at the time. To think that all this life can be chucked into a vast churning pool to be extruded into a giant algorithmic, generative sausage machine reduces so much so swiftly.'

Business teams are coming to terms with the need for governance on the use of generative AI. Some CEOs and risk officers have relayed that the use of this type of technology has been banned (or paused) in corporate environments. They are playing for time. Trying to hold back the tide and give some space and consideration to how to put guardrails in place.

The need to shore up security for business teams is growing. Recent research showed that people can detect a fake image only 60% of the time, and can detect how the image has been altered only 40% of the time.[45] Once we come to a place of generating images with AI how will our human brains cope? What tools do we have to evaluate what's human and not? The speed of generative AI and the pace at which it's making our lives smoother and more comfortable is, whilst very tempting, potentially leading us to a place of increasing homogeneity, and, therefore, less choice in real terms.[46]

---

44   Asmelash, L. (9 October 2023). 'These books are being used to train AI. No one told the authors.' *CTV News*. https://www.ctvnews.ca/sci-tech/these-books-are-being-used-to-train-ai-no-one-told-the-authors-1.6594068.

45   Nightingale, S, Wade, K & Watson, D. (2017). 'Can people identify original and manipulated photos of real-world scenes?' Cognitive Research: Principles and Implications. https://cognitiveresearchjournal.springeropen.com/articles/10.1186/s41235-017-0067-2.

46   Webb, A. (15-22 October 2023). Interview with Amy Webb. [Interview]. SXSW Sydney 2023. Sydney, New South Wales, Australia.

To keep pace with it all – and to support our future innovation – we may well need to use AI support. But we will also need to be both more critical of ideas and creative with the things that we use AI for.

The tech world that we live in plays a significant part in our own change management and we need to be aware of the impact (and usefulness!) of AI. How we manage the future of our organisation is dependent on the future of tech which has faced and is facing huge changes itself. But managing this is the only way to create new innovations and successfully implement change projects.

Environmental forces

Environmental changes are all over the news – a warming climate, the loss of habitats, the death of coral reefs, increasing tsunamis, cyclones and climate refugees... the list goes on. The damage we continue to cause to the home in which we live, or as we have grown accustomed to calling it, 'climate change', is gaining (very slowly) some momentum. New supply chain regulations in the European Union (EU) will come into effect in 2024. The EU is taking measures to meet targets to reduce carbon emissions as part of the 'Fit for 55 in 2030' package. A new regulation was introduced in 2023 to prevent the importation of commodities linked to deforestation with the intent to curb the loss of forests, biodiversity and land degradation.[47]

Resources on our planet are not infinitely renewable. The big question that troubles many of us is how to take the most impactful next step. Surely, at some point this must mean less consumption if we want to continue to keep our planet in a state that will support human life. If we allow that less consumption and more conscious consumption

47   Mark, E. (20 October 2023). 'How effective is the European Union's deforestation regulation?' East Asia Forum. https://eastasiaforum.org/2023/10/20/how-effective-is-the-european-unions-deforestation-regulation/.

are inevitable as circular economies evolve,[48] then the face of retail businesses and what they are concerned with also must shift. And so too our change projects.

Industry awareness

When it comes to change projects, most leaders will understand that industry awareness is vital.

The Economist Intelligence Unit has predicted that consumers will increase their patronage at physical stores in 2024 and beyond. This is driven by depleted household savings and continued cost of living pressure. 'Recovery in footfall at stores will encourage many retailers to expand their physical footprint in 2024 (even as many small businesses around the world shut down amid prohibitively high costs and interest rates).'[49]

Before we jump into expansion, we should also consider what's driving consumers. For some time we have been overpopulated with retail space.[50] During the pandemic years many conversations were had about re-deploying retail spaces to make use of them for health and as the 'third spaces' where communities come together. We are now entertaining more thoughts about what to do with underused office spaces as so many businesses have shifted to working in a hybrid mode.

When it comes to change projects, retail organisations need to consider the context of their customers and the overall shopping experience. Perhaps, rather than simply expanding their footprint, retailers should

---

48 Glenk, S. (14 May 2024). 'The Power of the Consumer.' SAP News Center. https://news.sap.com/2024/05/the-power-of-the-consumer/.

49 Economist Intelligence. Industry analysis: Consumer goods. EIU. https://www.eiu.com/n/consumer-goods-retail/.

50 Ayoub, J. 'Current challenges of the retail property market.' Raine & Horne Commercial.

reconsider their footprint and rethink how it might be used to attract customers, just as we're rethinking how to use retail space generally.

Global impacts on innovation

Global politics, economics, technology, environment, industry and demographics all play a part in why – the drivers – and how – the implementation – we bring change projects to life. With innovation clearly at risk around the world, growth is at risk too.

In order to really effectuate a change, we must make sure that every change project takes into account these global elements. This guides our project positioning, at least on a meta level.

Just as you would seriously consider taking on a change project to purchase a new brand during a recession, you might also seriously consider what your customers are looking for in terms of environmental packaging and your own environmental footprint. All of these elements will need to be part of your overall picture in order to create a successful change project.

Of course, we aren't only looking globally. More local elements will strongly play into your project positioning as well.

> In order to really effectuate a change, we must make sure that every change project takes into account these global elements.

Context drives change

If you're running a small retail business in the Southern Highlands, maybe some of these global or even local issues seem too broad to apply to your situation. But embracing growth means embracing change, and embracing change means looking to the future. That means that our change projects must consider both the current context and the future we may be operating in.

Your business, your team and your market matter – as do your country, your region and your world. The buying habits of your customers will impact how you market (TikTok or Google?) as well as the services and products you offer. The stability and cost of your supply chains will impact how much you can charge for new and current products. And whether or not you can repair the things you sell, or offer them in a more sustainable way, will certainly impact your ability to function into the future.

At a more global level, the economic context and political environment in which you're operating will impact your timing, your pace and even whether or not you proceed with a project. Environmental legislation happening overseas will filter through our Australian mindset and regulations and will drive future changes. Innovations and AI are rampant, and must be understood and adopted where needed – swimming against a swelling tide has never worked. From a corporate perspective, we need to build trust again with our customers and the broader world. Operating in the way we say we will and in a way that aligns with our customers' values and outlook on the world generally.

All this requires change. And to begin the change we first need to understand what success looks like for us, and how we can achieve it.

2

What we're trying to achieve (and what stops us from achieving it)

Change projects are a paradox. They're both special and mundane. They come into being when it's clear that we must change, improve, rethink or reshape but can't achieve what's required in the ordinary running of a business. To make necessary or desirable change requires additional effort and dedicated focus. So, the change project, by its very nature, sits outside the context of daily business needs and at the same time must serve the future strategy of the business. It must remain relevant and useful, even if that context shifts.

This is the paradox and duality of change projects.

Implementation brings us additional dualities. Projects are both a marathon and a sprint. They are both out of the ordinary and extraordinary. They require both distance from the day-to-day and the contributions of those who make the day-to-day happen. They form their own dedicated (borrowed) temporary teams and reshape the way teams are structured and work. They are fleeting in the life of a business and yet take up significant time and space. They start with the intent to improve and make our day-to-day business efforts easier, but are themselves often resource heavy. They are unique in time, context and intent, even when this 'same thing' has been done before.

Navigating these dualities successfully is no small feat. So to manage, you need to first pinpoint what you're *trying* to achieve. You need to understand what success looks like for your organisation, get a clear view of what may hold you back and determine what areas you need to focus on and actions you need to take to get you where you need to be.

What does success look like for you?

When you're starting a change project, one of the first questions always needs to be, 'what does success look like for your organisation? What will make a project successful *for you*?'

When I reflect on the clients I've worked with, there's one who stands out as having had a clear idea of what success would look like from the start of their project. Interestingly, for them real success revolved around what they wanted to *preserve* throughout the change.

One of the things they were very determined to preserve was their relationships with their customers. They were specific and clear about what made their customer relationships special and they were determined that these relationships would overarchingly still be ones that people valued and found both friendly and helpful.

During our meetings the client told stories about experiences customers had shared highlighting what was so good about their organisation. These stories gave them a solid grounding in what they already knew was working. No matter what we did on the process and systems side of things they were unshakably clear about what customers value about them and about what they needed to retain. Preserving the things that made them great, while implementing a change for the future, was success for them. This client understood what they needed to keep as well as what they wanted to change.

As you build the beginnings of your own project, consider what success looks like for you. To do this well, you also need to understand where you are right now.

Where are you?

Maybe you've been working on improvements to processes in your business, and now you've come to a point where questions about the right systems and tools are being asked. So you're looking to make a change and wondering how to implement it. Or you might be looking for a replacement system or considering how to transition to a new way of working or even a new business structure. You may have a project that's been on hold for a while that needs a restart. You may even be part way through a project that's not progressing to plan.

In each of these cases, you need to find out where you are before you begin to implement any changes. You might start by asking 'do we have the right tools for the job?' or 'do we have the right people?' You might also try asking 'what can we do better?' Or, 'where are we falling short?' The questions you ask yourself determine where you are in relation to that change and the steps that you'll need to take to strategise and implement changes that become a reality.

Collaboration and teamwork

Part of understanding where you are involves understanding how your team currently collaborates. Having a change team that collaborates well is the answer to a lot of the challenges that you will face, and the key to a smooth (or as smooth as possible) project. When you don't have this in place, it can significantly impact any success you might have envisaged.

So what do we mean by collaboration? There are probably as many versions of what collaboration is as there are those who attempt to practice it. When it comes to collaborative work practices, every business environment will have their own version of what this looks like. When we work with teams to implement technology and change we say:

Collaboration is where everyone who should contribute
is able to freely express opinions and views that
make the whole project (or process) better.

If this feels hard going, sometimes it's easier to define something by what it isn't. First, and most importantly, collaboration is not an invitation for personal attacks. When teams come together to work on projects and solve problems, the focus needs to be on the problem, no matter your personal level of frustration or exhaustion from any previous experiences. Creating safe environments where people can express themselves without fear of judgement or repercussions is key.

Secondly, the whole group is not required for every little thing. Have you ever watched a six-year-olds' game of football? They move in a pack, everyone wanting to be close to the ball. There is literally no one to pass to because all the players are packed so tight around the ball. People can interpret collaboration that way, but bringing an entire team to every single conversation is not collaboration. To me, this exhibits a lack of trust in the team or confusion about what part each team member should be playing.

Thirdly, collaboration is not a get together where everyone agrees, and we spend time validating an existing point of view or tearing down something without taking action. Different perspectives and approaches to the business build a richer picture of the work ahead, including dissenting opinions.

What we're looking to achieve is collaboration in its most useful state. This is teamwork that is open and emotionally tuned in. These are project members that have a clear understanding of why they are there, are playing to their strengths and are appreciating the strengths of other people on their team. This type of collaboration supports the efforts to raise the standard and improve how we're functioning together.

The collaboration continuum

It's helpful – when trying to determine where you are with collaboration – to think about it on a continuum. It appears in different forms in different businesses, but it also dynamically shifts within one business depending on the team, the purpose of your project and your efforts. Your team might move back and forth across this continuum through different activities and over time.

Within your team and even project, you may notice pockets of effective collaborative work and pockets that are less so. When you want to create momentum across a change project in business, your goal is to move through that continuum and focus your energy to build better collaborative practices in a more consistent way.

Effective collaboration is the key to success for your change project and it's this that we're trying to achieve. Effective collaboration and teamwork move people up the ladder from

Effective collaboration is the key to success for your change project and it's this that we're trying to achieve.

resistance (more on this later!), to cooperation, to high performance. So we need to start by doubling down on how our teams are evolving and working, and how we're collaborating and communicating, in all projects.

What are you bringing to the table?

You, as the project leader, set the tone for your change project. So it's in your interest to create the best environment possible for your team to thrive. That's why, when you're considering where you are at the start of a change project, it's a great idea to think about what you're bringing to the table. As part of the change process you'll be building new partnerships (for example, software vendors) and working relationships (for example, within the team). To have these work well you need to think about these partnerships and relationships like building a bridge. You need to build from both sides, with a clear understanding of where the bridge will meet in the middle.

To build a great bridge, with your vendor partners, for example, you need to consider if you are the type of team that:

- Value what they have to offer and who are prepared to share plans and aspirations so that the vendor can contribute.

- Own their part in changes and delays, and don't always look to 'kick the cat' (where the vendor partner is the cat).

- Take ownership and accountability for decisions that are made, rather than trying to offload responsibility for the decisions onto someone else.

- Make decisions in a timely manner, rather than leaving everything until the last second and then hoping the other partner can make a miracle happen.

- Share what they are trying to achieve, rather than assuming the 'solution' and telling the other party what it is.

- Communicate consistently and don't 'forget' to share changes of priority or direction.
- Give a clear brief about where they're trying to go and why.

Top down change versus bottom up change

We have often insisted that people are capable of extraordinary change. The thing that they don't typically like about change is that it's forced upon them. When it is, they will resist the change.

Fareed Zakaria, renowned political commentator, makes the same observation in the political arena in his book *Age of Revolutions*. In it he refers to several situations in political and social revolutions where the top-down imposition of new structures or ways of being on a national scale was completely and utterly ineffective.[51] On the face of it, there was the appearance of change. Underneath, the experience for most people was that their hearts were still elsewhere. And so, they were not able to embrace the change appropriately.

It can help to think of change in the same way you might think about your merchandising plan. Just like a merchandising plan needs both a top down and a bottom up view, so does change.

The top down view is: What are we aspiring to? Where do we want to stretch, evolve and improve?

The bottom up view is: What are we grounding ourselves in? What do we know won't change?

For one retail client, the top down was completely missing, and the project failed. The executive team had delegated the project without

---

51   Zakaria, F. (2024). *Age of Revolutions: Progress and Backlash from 1600 to the Present*. W. W. Norton & Company.

properly understanding their continuing responsibility to engage in the decision-making process and without ensuring that their teams had the time and space to make improvements. And so they simply weren't able to. Without the top down view, their efforts failed.

At another, the bottom-up efforts were being actively undermined with regional leaders positioning themselves and their stores in opposition to the new system changes, creating division in the project and consuming leadership focus and energy who were forced to de-escalate this situation rather than elevate and inspire the team. Again, without the bottom up view, the change needed suffered.

At a third 'Goldilocks' client, the team was able to strike a happy balance between top down and bottom up that was just right. People at the operational level were clear they needed to make changes. Senior leaders were also looking for how they could enable and support that change. It's this collaboration that we're striving for, what we're trying to achieve.

What holds us back from achieving change?

There are multiple things that get in the way; some of them are harder to see than others. It's a bit like renovating a house. It's obvious to me that I lack the skills to complete plumbing or carpentry to a standard that will satisfy the regulations to make a habitable building. However, it's easier for me to think that I can budget, project manage or design the desired renovation because I have some experience with these things in other situations. That doesn't mean that I can do it on a building project – or that I'll have the time and energy with all the other things I'm doing in my regular life. It's the same in the project situation. Most people have an understanding of the need to control a budget, but put those same people in a project environment alongside their everyday responsibilities, and it's easy for the project budget to be neglected.

How many of us have fallen into the trap of thinking that we can, with the same ease as a professional, complete a project budget or select the colours and finishes that will best suit our new environment?

The times when you need professionals are not when things are going well. It's when the unforeseen crops up and we need to figure out a plan under time (or budget) pressure. It's just like ripping up the floor and finding that everything is riddled with termites. It can get expensive quickly, but not addressing a termite problem in your foundations will build an unstable future structure. Make contingency plans for finding unexpected problems, but when it comes time to react or act, you'll want someone who's done it before along for the ride.

So while there are a wide range of unexpected things that can crop up along the path of a change project, making it hard for us to achieve, it's helpful to categorise them into two broad categories: technical and human.

Technical (and tangible)

The technical problems are the things you know you're not qualified for. Like carpentry and plumbing, these are more tangible and traceable, things like knowledge or skill gaps. To most, it's clear that they don't have the technical capability to be a solution architect or understand how an integration layer fits together or the best way to configure the new software. This is the domain of either the solution provider or their qualified implementation partner. The tangible things, like the detail of how your business manages products or inventory data or how it best serves its customers, are the realm of the business team experts. These two 'sides' of the project need each other to make a software implementation go well and need each other's experience and expertise to apply their skills and knowledge to create a successful implementation.

Human (relationships)

Then there are the more human things that get in our way, like the design and management sides of the project. Expectations need to be managed, this includes the expectations of the executives, but also the expectation of those in the 'doing layers' in the business. No matter what the expectations are, when we fall short, there is disappointment. Much of the time, businesses underestimate the amount that will be asked of them and their team. The business expertise doesn't sit with the software vendor; good ones will share what they know, but the onus to articulate all working processes sits with you on the business side.

So too do the expectations that you will test (deeply) the functionality of the software and manage the vendor to deliver. Product-led businesses intuitively understand the need for good supplier relationships but often miss putting the effort into this when dealing with software providers.

> Keeping expectations at a realistic level but still striving to achieve better is the constant state of the project.

Keeping expectations at a realistic level but still striving to achieve better is the constant state of the project.

Collaboration, teamwork, understanding what success means for you and having clarity over where you are at the start of a change project sets you up for success in achieving your change. But it's not always as simple as having those elements in place as there are challenges, both known and unknown, that will rise up along the way – that will hold us back from achieving your version of success – and you'll be in the position of herding those cats once again.

What's known versus what's unknown

When you're considering what might hold you back from achieving change in your organisation, you need to consider the challenges you know about (known challenges) but also challenges that you might not know about now (unknown challenges). It's a guarantee that every change project will face both.

In any change project, the project leads, contributors, sponsors, vendors and advocates will have a strong idea of where some challenges might arise. They might appear in the form of people who disagree with the purpose or process of implementing a project. It might be a funding dilemma. It might even come down to a timing challenge. But these challenges exist in the realm of what is known.

On the other hand, there will also be unknown challenges. These are things that can hold us back from making a change that we can't even conceptualise at the start of a change project, but that will certainly rear their heads at some stage. These unknown challenges are unidentified risks, and they've often been considered to be outside of the sphere of the project. But in reality, when you're running a change project, any unknown challenges will eventually make themselves known, and you will need to be prepared to handle them.

Known challenges may seem easier to manage since you can strategise a game plan from the start. But the real skill in change projects comes from being able to flexibly respond to all the challenges that will hold your project back from success, especially those that are unknown. Change projects require agile focus and flexible responsiveness.

Between a rock and a hairy choice (damned either way)

If you're struggling to get your project underway, you may find yourself caught between what feels like a rock and a hairy choice – or two horrible extremes.

On one side is the fear of not innovating; of stagnating and becoming irrelevant. Kodak, Nokia, Blackberry – there are plenty of examples of businesses that have neglected innovation at their peril. Ignoring technological changes can result in becoming obsolete, losing customers and, ultimately, shutting down. Blockbuster is one of the most cited examples of a company that failed to adapt to the digital transformation in the video rental industry. Its inability to foresee and embrace the shift towards streaming services, a significant technological innovation, contributed to its downfall.[52]

On the other side, there is the danger of innovation hubris that can lead enthusiastic players to bite off way more than they have capacity to chew. Take an example from the early 1990s. FoxMeyer, a leading pharmaceutical distribution company in the United States, embarked on an ambitious technology upgrade. The company invested in an SAP system and warehouse automation technologies, enlisting consultants for integration with the goal of enhancing operational efficiency. Originally budgeted at $35 million, this major IT initiative ended up contributing significantly to the company's collapse.

The project's failure stemmed from multiple factors. FoxMeyer aimed to overhaul its distribution systems within an aggressive 18-month timeline, a goal that proved to be overly ambitious. The threat of automation led

---

52   Downes, L & Nunes, P. (7 November 2013). 'Blockbuster Becomes a Casualty of Big Bang Disruption.' *Harvard Business Review*. https://hbr.org/2013/11/blockbuster-becomes-a-casualty-of-big-bang-disruption.

to resistance among warehouse staff, with the first warehouse rollout being met with sabotage, resulting in damaged stock and incomplete orders.

In addition, the new SAP system performance was disappointing. It handled only 10,000 orders nightly, a fraction of the 420,000 managed by the previous system. Compounding these issues, FoxMeyer contended that the consulting firm treated the project more as a training opportunity for novices rather than assigning experienced professionals, further exacerbating the project's challenges, and contributing to the company's downfall.[53]

Similar challenges have surfaced on projects I have worked on or next to. Everyone knows that this is difficult territory. Balancing the tension between the competitive forces of innovation, compelling us to upgrade and improve our technology, with the very possible pitfalls of projects requires some nerve. It's vital to properly prepare for any significant change project, including understanding your innovation appetite.

Moving towards collaboration is the key to success

The answer to many change problems is collaboration and high performance. This is how we improve and build momentum in our project teams. So within our change projects we need to focus on building better collaborative muscles – something often missing in cross-functional teams.

---

53   Scott, J. 'The FoxMeyer Drugs' Bankruptcy: Was it a Failure of ERP?' *The University of Texas at Austin.* https://zimmer.fresnostate.edu/~sasanr/Teaching-Material/MIS/ERP/FoxMeyer.pdf.

> **Collaborative practices build flow and speed – something that we refer to as momentum.**

Collaborative practices build flow and speed – something that we refer to as momentum. When the team is in a state of evolved collaboration they are working well together and progressing the work in a way that feels productive and positive. This doesn't mean that everyone has to agree. We need room for differences of opinion and debate.

Regardless of disagreement, collaborating teams are characterised by high levels of understanding and trust, clarity on the purpose of the project alignment and a well-matched pace. This state of momentum, to me, is more of an aspirational guide than anything as it's rarely 100% achievable. However, it's always helpful to have something to aspire to even if we often fall short of the ideal. I have worked in teams where momentum has been achieved for periods of time. But to achieve it we have to understand that the lynchpin of momentum is consistency.

Consistency builds momentum

Jim Collins in his oft cited book, *Good to Great,* describes the building of momentum by using the analogy of a flywheel.[54] A flywheel is used to smooth the fast angular velocity fluctuations of the crankshaft in a reciprocating engine. It's hugely useful, and hugely heavy. To get the heavy flywheel moving takes an immense amount of hard effort. It's not achieved by one single action; consistent effort is needed. However, once momentum kicks in, it's nearly unstoppable.

This analogy has a lot to offer to the project team looking to build a cooperative working practice. The essence of cooperation building is

---

54   Collins, J. (2001). *Good To Great.* CENTURY - TRADE.

consistency. It's unlikely that one intervention or action will make a big impression on the 'flywheel' of the project but consistent practice and improvements on the foundations will build momentum.

The Japanese practice of kaizen is 'based on the belief that continuous, incremental improvement adds up to substantial change over time.'[55] There are books and studies galore; from the entrenched business traditions of Steven Covey and his 'trim tab effect'[56] to the experiments of Gretchen Ruben[57]. So too it is with building cooperation into a project team. Small changes over the longer term build meaningful differences. Consistency builds momentum.

What does a collaborative culture feel like?

When I was a teenager, my mum had an operation on both her feet. During her recovery she would have to have both her feet in plaster and would not be mobile for some weeks. Dad would be running his own business and managing the home.

There are four of us kids. At the time we ranged in ages from mid-teens to primary school. Dad, in his usual methodical approach to life, developed, what was dubbed, 'operation cooperation'. It was a plan for us to step in and take on some of the things that Mum normally did, ourselves and cover the gap. Operation cooperation had clear roles and responsibilities, it had a timeframe and it had a lead up of mentally preparing four kids to take on a whole heap of additional chores that

55 Wilding, M. (22 January 2018.) 'The Japanese philosophy of Kaizen can reinvent your daily routine.' Quartz. https://qz.com/work/1183536/the-japanese-philosophy-of-kaizen-can-reinvent-your-daily-routine#:~:text=Put%20simply%2C%20the%20Kaizen%20approach,in%2Dhand%20with%20major%20innovation.
56 Covey, S. (2005). *The 8th Habit: From Effectiveness To Greatness*. Simon & Schuster.
57 Ruben, G. (2015). *The Happiness Project (Revised Edition): Or, Why I Spent a Year Trying to Sing in the Morning, Clean My Closets, Fight Right, Read Aristotle, and Generally Have More Fun*. Harper Paperbacks.

ranged from the uninteresting to the unwanted. There was a poster – a 'star chart' of sorts – where we were supposed to 'tick off' completed activities. This was a visual reminder and representation of the action plan.[58]

What has stuck many years later from 'operation cooperation' is the sense of creating a shared purpose to get through a period of transition. Reflecting on that now, as a leader of projects, one of the most striking things is how that spirit of cooperation, more than the hard facts of the roles, posters and intention, got us through. As much as the tools, methods, skills and tangible artifacts of project life are important, so too is this sense of shared cooperative effort to get to an objective or get through a transition.

How do we move toward collaboration?

For collaboration to really work in a project, the people who are working together must communicate effectively, share knowledge and be able to act. True collaboration requires a lot more emotional and social skills than real technical skills. Social skills are important because they encourage 'idea flow', building on ideas of the wider team and developing a practice of innovation.

Geoff Colvin, author of *Humans are Underrated*, cites research conducted by Alex Pentland of MIT Human Dynamics Laboratory, where participants wore tiny cameras on their clothes designed to pick up tone of voice and social interactions between the members and obscure the

---

58   My recollection is that the star chart ended up being tortured and possibly destroyed. Our aspirational selves were not able to deliver on all the promised virtues imagined at the beginning and the chart became a visual reminder of that failure.

actual words spoken.[59] The research found that team effectiveness is more correlated with social skills than anything else.

'Members of the very best teams did 3 things:

1. Generated many ideas with short contributions to conversation (no one went on at great length)

2. They engaged in 'dense interactions' advancing own ideas and contributing to the ideas of others

3. Everyone contributed ideas and reactions taking turns more or less equally (creating a wide diversity of ideas)

Everyone seems to think that ... leadership, mix of technical skills, vision, motivation - are more important. They matter, but not nearly as much as social skills.'

Social safety isn't enough – we need to elevate our standards too!

To bring our emotional best to a work stream or project the base layer of some level of psychological safety must exist. Amy Edmondson, who has led research on teamwork and psychological safety, says 'fostering a climate of respect, trust and openness in which people can raise suggestions without fear of reprisal. It's the foundation of a learning culture.'[60]

To create strong learning cultures, both high standards and high levels of psychological safety are needed. People must be both comfortable in making mistakes to learn, but also creating stretch targets to develop.

---

59 Colvin, G. (2016). *Humans are Underrated: What High Achievers Know That Brilliant Machines Never Will.* Portfolio.

60 Edmondson, A. Quoted in: Grant, A. (2 February 2021). *Think Again: The Power of Knowing What You Don't Know.* Viking.

Project work is often a vehicle for businesses to develop a more learning focused culture. To make a project successful the most capable people need to feel safe enough to contribute ideas and share knowledge with others. They need to feel confident that their contributions will be considered. They need to believe that their ideas matter and that they will be listened to. This requires leaders to build a team environment where everyone feels respected and trusted.

Some key skill sets that would be beneficial to develop in collaboration are:

1. Tolerance of others' views and capabilities, including being aware of different cultural contexts and being able to accept and control your own emotions.
2. Compromise, an ability to choose the best option for the goal or the project ahead the work we are to complete.
3. Reliability, the act of trusting that when a task is assigned or agreed upon that it will be completed.
4. Authenticity, bringing your own strengths to the table and respecting and recognising the strengths of others.

These are emotional and social capabilities that require application in a project team and propel the effectiveness and innovation in a team ahead.

What does effective collaboration look like in practice?

Constructive collaboration involves conflict, or task-focused conflict, which is debate and difference about the best approach or outcome.

It can be heated and at times awkward or challenging but it doesn't descend into name calling or personal attacks. People can disagree and feel frustrated, but it shouldn't get personal. Instead constructive collaboration provides insight.

My own lived experience on one project team recently has shown much push and pull about the fastest and best approaches for various elements of the project. This debate and discussion has, at times, been difficult to engage with as there've been parties who are very committed to their particular view of the outcome. But it's been worth it in the end.

This debate and discussion has actually led to better collaboration, and often we've found ourselves working in a way that aligns with my original definition – namely that collaboration is where everyone who should contribute is able to freely express opinions and views that make the whole project better.

When you have collaboration and consistency, you have momentum and times of high performance, and both of these are vital for your ultimate success. But this is just the beginning. Now you need to undertake the change itself.

The 4 areas for change

Cross functional collaboration is the way that we can speed up the delivery of that change and the purpose behind the change. There's no one path to making a team great, making it work and taking it into high performance. Instead, there are many good ways to do these things. But here, we're going to focus on four that I've found to be the most efficient at helping teams move up the scale to the nirvana of smooth collaboration:

1. Strategy
2. Alignment
3. Transparency
4. Accountability & communication

It's these four areas that we'll be focusing on in the rest of the book, to offer suggestions, insights and tips that will drive you and your team into high performance. The suggestions and experiences offered here are the hard-won insights from years of experience working with clients to develop better practices and deliver changes with greater impact and speed. And I believe they can do the same for you.

At the end of the day, everyone can change.

> "Find a group of people who challenge and inspire you, spend a lot of time with them, and it will change your life."
>
> – Amy Poehler

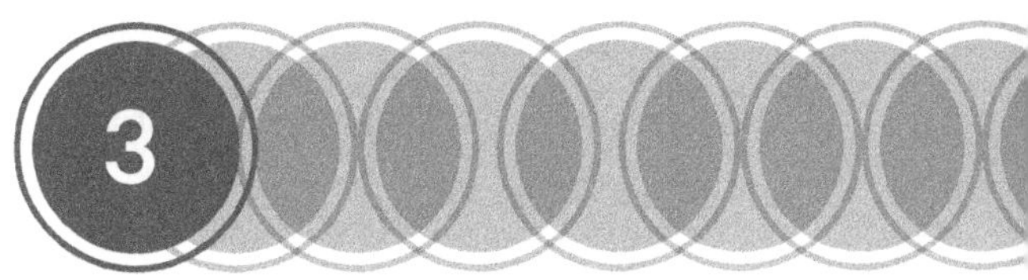

3

Strategy

If everyone can change, then every organisation can implement a change project. But delivering a project that is collaborative, that has the underpinning of a high-performing team and is therefore efficient and purposeful, is the goal. To achieve that takes a firm grasp of strategy.

What is strategy in a change project context?

Strategy defines what you don't do, as much as what you do. Or as one article on the topic said it is 'the "above the shoulders" work that focuses on prioritising tradeoffs for creating value or mitigating risk. Intentionally choosing what to do is just as important as choosing what not to do.'[61]

To me, strategy is future facing (with some reflection on the past). One dictionary says that 'good strategy provides a clear roadmap with guiding principles or rules to define actions for achieving these goals.'[62]

61   Bucci, A. (21 March 2020). 'Personal Growth and Prof' Galloway's Strategy Sprint.' *Anthony Bucci Blog.* https://www.anthonybucci.com/personal-growth-and-prof-galloways-strategy-sprint/.

62   Merriam-Webster. (n.d.). Strategy. In Merriam-Webster.com dictionary. https://www.merriam-webster.com/dictionary/strategy.

A relatively simple definition of strategy can be determining how we win in the period ahead.

Strategic goals for a whole business ideally are like a nesting set of matryoshka dolls. Each goal builds alignment to the strategy from the executive level to the management level to the action level in the organisation, ensuring that everyone is working to achieve the same strategic outcome. This lines up with our definition – determining how to win in the period ahead.

As you might have experienced, management consultants[63] and experts often have different takes on how to best develop strategy. Whether you've used Porter's Five Forces, which is great for understanding external competition, the BCG Matrix which helps with product lifecycle or the McKinsey 7S model which focuses on internal alignment, each framework offers unique insights and the best choice depends on what aspect of strategy you need to focus on.

In every case, strategy is situation dependent. For example, in some businesses, operational ways of working are strategic, particularly if they create a competitive advantage or build a moat around the business. (McDonalds and Amazon are great examples of businesses who have taken operational execution to a level of competitive advantage.) In others, operational ways of working may not lead to strategic outcomes, but may simply be day-to-day activities.

Regardless, strategy for all retail businesses must be future facing and serve the customer. When we talk about being 'in service' to the customer, it's the word service that should be our guide, including guiding our

---

63   Gratton, P. (18 June 2024). 'Porter's Five Forces Explained and How to Use the Model.' Investopedia. https://www.investopedia.com/terms/p/porter.asp; Stanke, B. (4 February). 'A Comprehensive Guide to Strategic Planning Models.' Bob Stanke. https://www.bobstanke.com/blog/strategic-planning-models.

strategy. Serving customers means meeting their needs and wants. And serving customers strategically means anticipating their needs and wants and implementing this at the heart of your organisational change strategy.

Adopting a customer-centric change strategy

When it comes to undertaking any change project, there is one person that must be at the centre of your strategy – and that's your customer.

Many (all) of our projects embrace some form of new technology. But technology for its own sake is at best a novelty and at worst an annoyance. Customers quickly get bored with it if it doesn't deliver some value for them. Post pandemic we have witnessed multiple retailers reorganise themselves to orient back towards stores, removing or reducing services, such as video shopping and virtual try-ons, that were designed to connect with customers when face-to-face shopping was exponentially more difficult. Click and collect remains for the most part but this still puts a lot of work on the customer.

Today, 84% of retail transactions still take place in a store.[64] Browsing, searching and researching are at your fingertips via the phone in your pocket, but the joy of touching, feeling and trying as well as learning something you didn't already know about a product or brand comes better from physical stores.

A colleague recently related an experience in the Nike store in NYC. He shared that on entering the store he had downloaded the app, then used it to review and look at products, find the one he was interested

---

64   Wang, S et al. (20 January 2022). 'Why Do Some Consumers Still Prefer In-Store Shopping? An Exploration of Online Shopping Cart Abandonment Behavior.' *Frontiers in Psychology.* https://www.ncbi.nlm.nih.gov/pmc/articles/PMC8811303/#:~:text=Data%20shows%20that%2084%25%20of,sellers%20(Marian%2C%202021).

in and have it brought to him to try on. His size was not available in the store, but he was able to purchase it and the item in question was at his home before he returned. A completely seamless integration of technology into the customer purchase flow.

Contrast this with the recent experience of my partner in Sydney. Having purchased with a certain retailer previously (a suit) he went back to the retailer to look for business shirts. The shirt he was interested in was not available in his size. The Sydney store told him. that he could go online and buy it for himself. But as he was relating this experience to me he shared that he hadn't bought it yet. Why not? He hadn't gotten around to it. He ultimately bought several shirts direct from the manufacturer online, and bypassed the retailer altogether.

Instead of the DIY approach imagine the option where the retail assistant helps the customer to select shirts based on fabric and fit (even if the desired ones are not available) and adds them to a shopping cart in store sending him a link to review and pay or better yet having him pay in store and they ship to him! How much of a better technology experience would that have been, for both the customer and the retailer? I know that I'm on the NYC side of things. (This is not to say there aren't great retailers in Sydney. These are just two recent examples that are great comparison points.)

Follow the customer and you'll never look for growth.[65] This adage holds true here too. Keeping the customer at the heart of what you're doing is the key to delivering any change projects – including technology projects – that add value to your business and team. Whilst much of the technology tools we work on in our daily practice relates to the back end of businesses, there still must be a result that makes the business better for the customers.

---

65   A truism that I have tried to find an origin for but cannot.

Determining your own organisation's customer-centric change strategy means diving into your data with the goal of gaining insight or 'foresight' into your customers. Foresight has been defined as 'data-backed, quantitative models, compelling narratives about plausible futures.'[66]

Seeing the plausible futures for your organisation is the underpinning of any change project. Unfortunately, leaders today are not often getting the right information. Amy Webb, American futurist, author and founder and CEO of the Future Today Institute, believes that strategy has uncoupled itself from foresight in recent decades and makes a strong argument for the mutual benefit we gain from both. 'Strategy without foresight makes companies vulnerable to outside disruption. Foresight without strategy renders scenarios unactionable.'[67]

But whether it's called insight or foresight or simply analysis, it's the science and art of posing questions and looking for patterns in the data that lead to greater understanding of your customer. We must be doing this analysis when developing our change strategies, because without this connection, we're not going to be able to drive customer-centric change.

Change strategies must be forward looking & grounded in PURPOSE

Projects are the vehicles of possibility. They are born from strategic directives and are, in many situations, the work needed to deliver future wins for your business. The work of strategic projects closes the gap between actual and aspirational, allowing you to reach for a purpose outside of the regular day-to-day of the business they exist

---

66   Webb, A. (12 January 2024). 'Bringing True Strategic Foresight Back to Business.' *Harvard Business Review.* https://hbr.org/2024/01/bringing-true-strategic-foresight-back-to-business.

67   Webb, A. Bringing True Strategic Foresight Back to Business.

Everything within
a change project
is built on the
foundation of a
clearly articulated
purpose of
the project.

within. But in order to close the gap between actual and aspirational you must understand the purpose. Everything within a change project is built on the foundation of a clearly articulated purpose of the project. It's this articulated purpose that gives you the thing to strive for – it becomes the forward looking driver.

Purpose is not the same as outcome – and purpose cannot be encapsulated by KPIs alone. Purpose is the guiding light behind the outcomes we seek. It's the bridge between what we aspire for and the practical, implementable actions it will take to get us there.

Purpose also thrives in cooperative teams. Supported with the right skills, incentives and resources and guided by a plan of action the group that is cooperating and understands their purpose has created a shared understanding of what they're here for.

'Arguably, the most important job a leader has in a crisis is to consistently articulate this purpose and connect each day's tasks to it.'[68] I agree. Purpose is a fundamental need of project and business teams and a fundamental part that leaders must play.

In most cases, the people that are involved in your project – those responsible for its conception and implementation – will be able to articulate the purpose, but it's not always true in those teams that are a little way removed. The best case scenario is that everyone in

---

68   Groysberg, B & Abrahams, R. (17 August 2020). 'What the Stockdale Paradox Tells Us About Crisis Leadership.' *Harvard Business School*. https://hbswk.hbs.edu/item/what-the-stockdale-paradox-tells-us-about-crisis-leadership.

the organisation can articulate the project's purpose in a similar way. Where this doesn't happen, the next best case situation is that they, at the very least, display good will and good intent towards the project even if they don't understand its ultimate purpose. In that situation, however, the leaders of the project must frequently check in to ensure that good will continues. If not, you'll start getting the snide comments and asides that can begin to undermine the project overall.

Of course, often our aspirational purpose is easier to conceptualise than to achieve. Whilst possibility and purpose are the core of what motivates a team, we must also be present to, and address, the limitations of whatever current reality we find ourselves in.

The Stockdale paradox, first coined by Jim Collins[69] and named after the quote from James Stockdale below, articulates this tension between optimism and reality. It's the balance to strike when leading in difficult situations.

> 'You must never confuse faith that you will prevail in the end — which you can never afford to lose — with the discipline to confront the most brutal facts of your current reality, whatever they might be.'
>
> James Stockdale

We must have faith but confront reality. At its heart, this balance of possibility and grounded 'taking stock' of the reality of current existence is the best mindset to bring to project work.

---

69 Collins, J. Good to Great.

Change strategies must prepare you for crises

'Here's a sobering truth that most C-suites won't acknowledge: Considering the speed at which most modern companies are reasonably capable of moving (read: laboriously slow compared to the rate of external change), by the time a two-year plan is executed, the future will have moved further out of reach. Strategy's mission-critical responsibility — to chart a clear organisational direction and follow through with a robust execution plan — is being overridden by the immediate pressures of resource allocation and everyday operational tactics.' [70]

Despite its described limitations, strategy is vital for future proofing your organisation, whether you're engaged in a change project or not. Strategy is like taking an umbrella out on a walk. If you have one, you're ready for the rain (and it might be just me but when I remember to take one, I rarely need it). But if you don't take one, you will undoubtedly find yourself caught in a downpour.

In the same way, if you at least assume that there will be a crisis moment at one point (or many points) through the project, then you'll prepare a game plan for how to get out of it. If you go in without giving it consideration it will derail the project at just the wrong moment. Thinking ahead for what may go wrong is a useful exercise and can uncover risks that you'll want to manage as part of your project.

Google uses the 'writing a press release' approach to strategy at the beginning of every project.[71] This is a forward-thinking technique used to envision the successful completion and impact of a project. It helps

70   Webb, A. Bringing True Strategic Foresight Back to Business.
71   Collected by Google. Core Method: Future Press Release. Design Sprints. https://designsprintkit.withgoogle.com/methodology/phase2-define/future-press-release.

identify the project's goals and potential challenges from the outset by forcing the team to consider the end state and success criteria.

Atlassian, on the other hand, has a practice of conducting a pre-mortem before every change project.[72] This involves team members imagining that a project has failed and working backwards to determine what might lead to this failure. This approach helps identify potential risks and mitigation strategies before they become actual issues.

These issues-focused strategies are just two useful techniques for thinking through what might go wrong and preparing your metaphorical umbrella. Getting these thoughts out of heads and using the power of the team to create a plan of attack for when we need it will serve you well.

How to create your change strategy

All strategy is situation specific. There's no one way to create strategy and there's no one place to look for the resources and data you need to create it. Nonetheless, there are some driving forces that should help you to mould your own specific strategy within your organisation's project. And it begins with understanding exactly what *shouldn't* change.

Start with what to keep

Zakaria puts forward some fascinating observations on revolutionary changes and how they transpire (or not). One of his observations is that to allow space for significant changes and for them to evolve without

---

72   Welbon, C. (29 April 2019). 'Using premortems to calm your nerves and nail that big project.' Atlassian. https://www.atlassian.com/blog/teamwork/why-premortem-analysis.

bloodshed, humans need to be clear about what is being conserved or retained.

Most of his examples are working over decades rather than the shorter timeframes we're often focused on in software and process change projects. However, this extended timeframe, and distance from the events allows us to observe (with lovely hindsight) how when the right things are conserved and protected within an organisation changes may be enacted without carnage.

In other words, to be confident in making giant steps towards change, there must be a solid ground of things that stay the same, the things that the organisation should and must keep doing. This is your conservation strategy.

When I talk about this idea with clients and customers, I often ask them what won't change. This is an often-practised question in agile methodology, asking 'What should we keep doing?' When doing this in your own organisation, this practice forces you to examine what you're currently doing and look for where it's succeeding. It forces you to pinpoint the things that shouldn't change.

Of course, this is not an easy thing for humans to do. We are hardwired to notice threats and changes in our environment that might be detrimental, but rarely do we take a moment to notice what does work. When changes are first put forward most people intuitively want to answer the internal questions: why are we doing this; what does it mean for me; and what will it look like when we're done? It's part of assessing the risk to ourselves and the level of expected difficulty involved in making the change.[73]

---

73 Anderson, E. (7 April 2022). 'Change Is Hard. Here's How to Make It Less Painful.' *Harvard Business Review.* https://hbr.org/2022/04/change-is-hard-heres-how-to-make-it-less-painful.

Focusing on 'what to keep' helps identify and preserve the core strengths of an organisation. This can maintain morale and preserve effective practices.[74] Highlighting what will remain constant can help reduce employee anxiety and resistance to change. By acknowledging what works well, organisations can provide a sense of stability, which makes the transition smoother.[75]

Adopt ongoing refinement

Understanding your conservation strategy is the first step. But then it's time to begin pushing at the metaphorical flywheel. Remember, to get the flywheel going takes hard effort, and consistent action is needed. But once you get it moving, you will gain momentum. And as teams build familiarity and social bonds, they develop capacity for greater psychological safety. Psychological safety paired with a commitment to excellence will soon lead to a culture conducive to learning[76] (and, therefore, a culture conducive to change and growth). This learning stage is refinement.

Refinement is sometimes referred to as 'continuous improvement' or kaizen, which we touched on briefly earlier. The word kaizen translates to 'good change'. Kaizen is less about hustle and working more, and more about thoughtful adjustments, accepting failure and applying learnings. Its intent is to drive change through consistently applying thought and reflection on how to improve instead of pushing through one big upheaval. It's the ultimate nirvana of a learning culture. It's also the next step in your strategy for change.

---

74 Cameron, E & Green, M. (2024). *Making Sense of Change Management: A Complete Guide to the Models, Tools and Techniques of Organizational Change.* Kogan Page.

75 Kotter, J. (2012). *Leading Change.* Harvard Business Review Press.

76 Edmondson, A. (2018). *The Fearless Organization: Creating Psychological Safety in the Workplace for Learning, Innovation, and Growth.* John Wiley & Sons.

Develop your direction (slowing down to speed up)

Whether you're navigating out of the mess of resistant behaviour or setting the scene for the start of a project, it's essential that there's a clear and concise purpose to set the direction of the project. And, as discussed above, this purpose will drive the direction of your strategy. However, developing clear (and smooth) direction (and the subsequent momentum) often requires us to slow down.

As Jocko Willink, American author, podcaster and retired United States Navy officer and a former member of Navy SEAL Team 3, says, 'Slow is smooth and smooth is fast.' While most of us will never find ourselves in the types of extreme situations that elite Navy SEALs do, there is value in understanding this approach to challenges brought on by change. In our case, we might think of it as 'slow down and clarify'.

Sitting in front of a computer is not what most people would refer to as a physically demanding job; it lacks the danger associated with mining, physical labour or Navy SEALs reconnaissance missions. Still it can wear you down. At the end of 2023, I was tired and in pain, I had constant pain in my neck and arms from working in front of a screen.

A chance change of routine had me, one morning close to Christmas, with a different trainer at the gym from my usual guy. The new guy had a different approach. He didn't breeze through the steps or chat. He consulted with the tablet and had me do the usual weights that the program dictated but he watched me from a good couple of steps away – intently.

Really intently.

He studied me from every angle as I did the first set of weights. He corrected my technique in minute detail; shoulders down, elbows up, abs on, breathe in, breathe out, look ahead, relax your neck... it was like listening to a yoga teacher.

He took weight off the machine and made me slow down, forcing me to focus not on powering through but on doing each exercise well and in the way it was intended. After the session I knew that this was what I needed. Sure enough, by the end of January, after a couple of weeks off for a holiday and different training routine, the pain in my neck was gone.

I have said to clients many times in projects that often you need to slow down and clarify before you can speed up. What that means is that you need to focus on technique and improving the way you're operating rather than spending energy 'powering through'. Often the intent and energy of that powering through means we miss elements that are being executed poorly in haste.

Hastily executed work is often mistake laden or incomplete. What this means for downstream receivers of your work effort is that they then need to come back to correct or clarify for them to execute their part. This creates frustration and distrust in a group. On the other hand, doing it once and well is more satisfying for everyone involved, but to do so requires focus on technique and attention to the basics like in my training experience.

The key thing here is to make sure that everyone knows what the end goal (the purpose) is and why it matters. If you don't communicate the end goal well, your team won't know whether they're making progress towards it. The end goal drives the direction – but it's the slowing down, reviewing the steps and the work produced, that ensures you're travelling in the right direction.

Define your team

Foundation building is a future investment. And there's no more important foundation than your change team. At the strategy level we're focused on pulling together a base level team that can work effectively on the project as envisioned at the time. Ultimately, our goal is to achieve a collaborative team that strives as one to achieve the change project and its ultimate purpose. But in the beginning, we need a more directive approach – that is, decisions driven by one or two (or so) key people – that allows a transition to building teamwork and collaboration in your project.

An idea shared is the beginning for a project. A small group, (even just two people) who are clear what the potential business benefits are is enough. While traditional project management approaches recommend having a single project sponsor, lived experience has shown me that having two sponsors can be successful, particularly for large, complex projects. A little research has also produced some recent examples of infrastructure projects where this works too.[77]

In retail businesses the level of complexity is not the same as infrastructure, but there's still benefit in different strengths coming together to build projects. Those who are clear about the business benefits and have the vision and capacity to champion should be the project sponsor(s). It's critical to have a sponsor who both believes in the ultimate benefits the project will realise and who can stay the course

---

77   The South Eastern Program Alliance (Level Crossing Removal Program) is one example, sponsored by The Victorian Government (providing funding and overall direction) and The Level Crossing Removal Project (LXRP) organization (managing delivery). South Eastern Program Alliance (Level Crossing Removal Program). [Case Study]. Bis Oxford Economics. https://www.constructors.com.au/wp-content/uploads/2020/11/ACA-IA-Response-South-Eastern-program-Alliance.pdf.

when things don't go to plan. They must be clear about what's required, by when and the quality and standards to meet.

This includes providing clarity on ways of working, timeline expectations, communication channels, where skill gaps are and how change and risk will be managed. These may not all be intuitively understood by the key directors in the beginning but must be developed as part of giving the project enough structure that it will function well.

The most obvious example of directive forms of leadership is in the defence forces. Here the 'command and control' leadership style has traditionally been the fastest path to action in high-stakes situations like combat.

This form of directive project decision making places a lot of onus and responsibility on one or a very small group of people. If these leaders are ones with vision and compassion, we can build from the directive approach out to a more networked and cooperative team where we develop autonomy and communication that reduces dependence on a centralised command style.

Understanding who should take on the additional team roles, and how to divide those responsibilities is the next step.

There are reams of documents out in the world on how to define roles, what roles are required for different project methodologies and how to put this together. Like software not fixing a problem on its own, a clear role description doesn't solve everything until the people who are in those roles start doing the work.

Often the client thinks that if they engage external expertise, they can dilute their own roles and responsibilities. It's not so. Fundamentally a client needs to think about this as their baby. No matter how great the gap between their current knowledge and the vendor's expertise, the client will always be the expert on their own business. When the project is finished it's their team who will inherit the change (processes and technology). So, they need to know how it works, what can and can't be changed and be aware enough to know when to ask for help.

Once you have your roles designated, you must also work to agree between all the parties which methods will be used and how working together will flow. Each person must understand their role, what they are responsible for and who they need to work with to complete those responsibilities. Ensure that everyone is clear on the terms of engagement and the deadlines that have been set. Discuss and clarify how you can escalate any issues that can't be resolved and what types of checks and guardrails are needed to keep the project and team on track.

68 Prepare for success by planning for failure

Your strategy is designed to deliver success. But the best way to prepare for success is by planning for failure. Looking again at Google's 'writing a press release practice' can give us some insight on how to begin a project. The exercise asks the team to write the press release for their finished project. This forward imagining helps get clarity on the value that will be provided and asks for some tangible measures to share.

Then do the Atlassian 'pre-mortem' sometimes called a 'reverse post mortem'. What can go wrong with the imagined project? Getting people to think about that helps to anticipate potential failure points. A similar approach is adopted by the Australian cricket team captain Pat Cummings. He asks the question of the team 'how do you want to fail today?' Asking the question of 'how' do you want to fail frees up the often back of mind fear of failing to stop thinking 'will I fail' but 'how will I fail', and leads to the opportunity to consider failure productively.

Cummings describes how the Australian team typically chooses to fail by 'swinging hard'. In other words they fail by bringing their best selves to the game, taking risks that lean into their strengths and backing themselves to give their all. If they fail from this place, they will know that they've given what they have and have not held back or been too timid to take risks.

Change projects can be like large and stretching swings. But if we understand the risks, we can back our team through them. Implementing solutions to possible failure points must be part of your change project strategy.

Collaborate to the end goal

The final step of your strategy should be how you are going to move into a collaborative team process and culture. Part of this will be to establish what a collaborative team looks like for you and for your project. To achieve this you'll have to establish some basics, including setting out a clear project purpose, defining the roles, working requirements and how to approach problems and the scope of the project and the timeline for completion. You will also have 'agreed to' ways of working and the team will have demonstrated that they are able to navigate shared documents and working processes.

Finally, approval, change and risk processes must be defined for all, they must not be too onerous or bureaucratic, and reporting progress against agreed targets and milestones must be understood by all members of the project team.

With the basics understood, cooperation can be built with everyone working on the project.

It's important to include how you will create a cooperative culture as part of your strategy because cooperative cultures can move projects forward at a more significant rate than teams who are being directed. Instead of waiting for, or needing, direction, the cooperative project group develops autonomy and knows who to connect with and what to ask for to keep building momentum.

Is your project in alignment with your business?

A well-devised change strategy isn't just a standalone plan. It's an integral part of your organisation's overall vision and goals. It begins with a focus on what should stay the same – and in every organisation, much should remain – then moves through the strategic process of team building, purpose finding and direction achieving.

In essence, the strategy serves as a bridge between the present and the future, between where you are now and where you want to be once your change has been implemented. It will guide the project team through challenges and opportunities with a clear sense of purpose while also fortifying the entire business against the uncertainties of the future.

Of course, the strategy is only as good as its implementation, and to achieve that requires a collaborative and high performing team. And to achieve that, you need alignment.

For every project team that we build, our focus must be on what we call the 'triple A' elements – these are alignment, action and accountability.

We need alignment before taking action, and to keep ourselves on track with the action taken, accountability must be baked in. These embrace the vital elements of strategy, transparency and communication, each of which are explored in detail in later chapters.

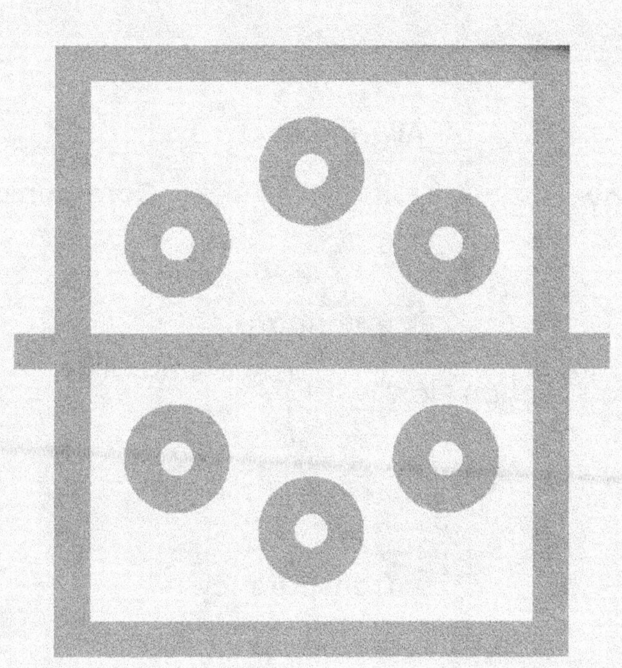

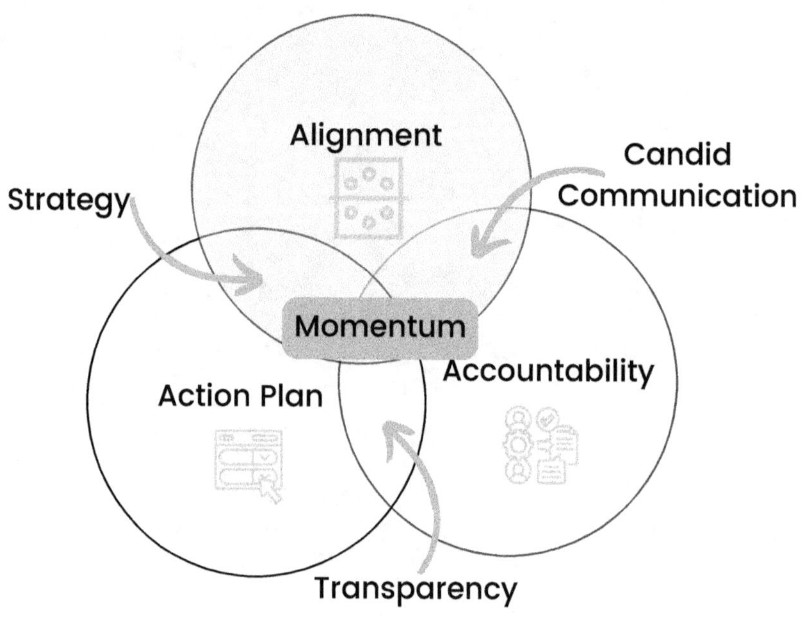

Strategy
Alignment
Candid
Communication
Momentum
Action Plan
Accountability
Transparency

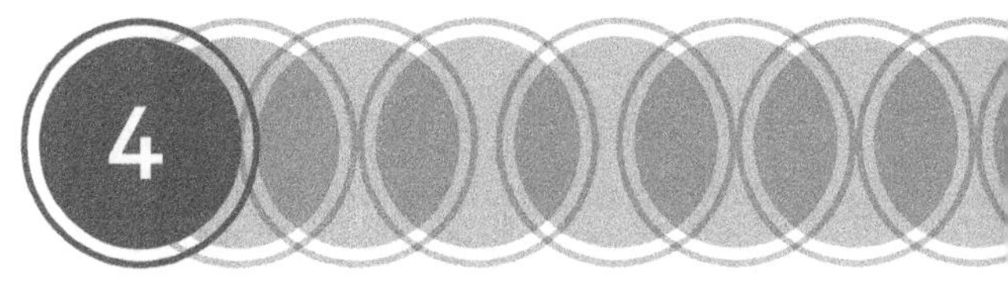

Alignment

In a 2021 article *Harvard Business Review* presented research indicating that 3 to 5% of people contribute approximately 30% of the additional momentum that we gain from cross functional efforts in project teams and work.[78] So just 5% of people provide a 30% uptick. I like to think of these people as the 'extra milers'. Those who contribute so much more than their colleagues to the ultimate results of a project.

What makes someone an 'extra miler'? This group of specialists usually have a 'day job' and are people who naturally look for opportunities to improve and work with others to develop better practices or ways of working. They are information hubs and subject matter experts – people who others gravitate towards to understand information, find hidden data or connect the dots on processes they don't understand. These people are the magnets to which iron filings are attracted.

But when you have a core group of people contributing more, it also can feel like an unfair distribution of work. Is this just an unreasonable effort falling on a few well-intentioned souls who are prepared to carry

78 Cross, R, Rebele, R & Grant, A. (January - February 2016). 'Collaborative Overload: Too much teamwork exhausts employees and saps productivity.' *Harvard Business Review.* https://hbr.org/2016/01/collaborative-overload.

the load and make the connections across functional areas that we need? Perhaps. However, through another lens, we can also see it as the power of a small group of *aligned* people to make real change in an organisation. These are people that are truly converted to the purpose of the project; that understand the need, the outcomes being sought and the drivers that will get the organisation there.

What the extra milers show us is that you don't need to convince everyone that change is needed. The right group – the aligned group – can make a difference. In fact, it takes only 10% of a group with an unshakeable belief to create an influence on the remaining part of that group.[79] And it takes only 25% of a workforce to commit to a change to create momentum across a business.[80]

When I think about this research, it brings to mind the well known quote from Margaret Mead:

> 'Never doubt that a small group of thoughtful, committed, organised[81] citizens can change the world; indeed, it's the only thing that ever has.' – Margaret Mead[82]

Of course I looked up this quote, and of course that led to a bunch more questions about its origins. As uplifting and inspiring as I find it, I can find no primary evidence that it came from Margaret Mead herself.

---

79   Rensselaer Polytechnic Institute. (26 July 2011). 'Minority rules: Scientists discover tipping point for the spread of ideas.' ScienceDaily. www.sciencedaily.com/releases/2011/07/110725190044.htm.

80   Damon Centola et al. (2018). 'Experimental Evidence for Tipping Points in Social Convention.' *Science*. https://www.science.org/doi/10.1126/science.aas8827.

81   The word 'organised' is often omitted from this quote.

82   Quote Investigator. (12 November 2017). 'Never Doubt That a Small Group of Thoughtful, Committed Citizens Can Change the World; Indeed, It's the Only Thing That Ever Has.' https://quoteinvestigator.com/2017/11/12/change-world/.

Despite its unclear origins, I have seen this in practice in organisations myself. The alignment of a small group of people to the core of a project's purpose can build momentum and create a movement within a business that drives the entire business forward.

The benefits of alignment to purpose

Purpose is not a poster on a wall. It's not a meme or a mantra. It's a deeply rooted insight into what matters in your organisation.

Ranjay Gulati, organisational scholar and Professor of Business Administration at the Harvard Business School, has dedicated significant time to studying purpose-led businesses and the leaders that develop them. His work around 'deep purpose' shows that capable leaders embed purpose and vision in the daily actions that they take. Gulati's work contributes to the idea that organisations with a clear purpose at their heart make it easier for their staff to align and sense check their own day-to-day working with the business.[83]

This alignment to purpose also drives other benefits, including building better boundaries, creating a sense of belonging, lifting performance and even fueling greater effort from the team as a whole.

Purpose creates boundaries

Priya Parker, a conflict resolution strategist and author of *The Art of Gathering: How We Meet and Why It Matters*, tells us that purpose can even help us create boundaries and acts as a helpful decision-making

---

83   Gulati, R. (2022). *Deep Purpose: The Heart and Soul of High-Performance Companies*. Harper Business.

tool about who to include in the project. Her guiding principle is that purpose should be 'specific, unique and disputable'.[84]

Purpose builds a sense of belonging

To Parker, purpose is grounded in 'what it means to you'. A business team I once worked with named their project after a bowl of noodle soup. It made no sense in any other context or to any other person. However, to this group of people, at this point in time, for this project, it said something.

The project name highlighted the purpose *for that team*, and for that reason, it worked.

Brené Brown's research on belonging offers valuable insights that can be applied to building a shared purpose during organisational change. Brown's concept of 'true belonging' encourages people to be their authentic selves. If we can harness authenticity it can lead to more candid feedback and creative problem-solving during change initiatives. When people feel they belong, they're more likely to take ownership of the change process, leading to a more collaborative approach.[85]

Purpose lifts performance

Performance and sports psychologist Dr Jim Loehr, spent years researching and developing tools and techniques for sportspeople to improve their capability and what he calls their mental toughness.[86] He

84   Parker, P. (2018). *The Art of Gathering: How We Meet and Why It Matters.* Riverhead Books.

85   Brown, B. (11 September 2017). 'Finding our way to true belonging.' Ideas.Ted.com. https://ideas.ted.com/finding-our-way-to-true-belonging.

86   Parrish, S. (Host). (30 April 2024). 'Dr. Jim Loehr: Change the Stories You Tell Yourself.' (No. 193) [Audio podcast episode]. In *The Knowledge Project.* https://podcasts.apple.com/au/podcast/the-knowledge-project-with-shane-parrish/id9901494811?i=1000654006819.

observed a marked difference between those who have an underlying driving purpose and those who don't. He attributes that deeper purpose as the difference that helps athletes complete what it was that they had set out to do.

In one interview, he relates the story of Andre Agassai,[87] who rebuilt his tennis career after significant setbacks, and connects this success back to the purpose that Agassi found off the court in the charitable work he was doing at the time. The tennis star had found that in working for others he was fuelled by purpose. This brought a lightness to his playing that counteracted the weight of expectations he felt otherwise.[88]

The same can be said of our teams and team members. A sense of purpose and the joy that comes from working from intrinsic motivation often lifts performance.

Purpose fuels discretionary effort

We already know that a small group of aligned workers can drive success in your project. And that's because the work of projects depends heavily on what we call discretionary effort.

Discretionary effort represents the extra energy, time and commitment that team members willingly invest in their jobs because they are motivated, engaged and committed to the success of the project. Discretionary effort often leads to increased productivity, higher-quality work and improved overall performance.

87   AQR International. (19 May 2024). Talking Toughness with Dr Jim Loehr (Part One). [Video file]. YouTube. https://www.youtube.com/watch?v=dyxOfHGN3OM.

88   McCraw, D. (1 June 2107). 'Andre Agassi: From 1 to 141 and Back Again.' Nordic Business Forum. https://www.nbforum.com/nbreport/andre-agassi-from-1-to-141-and-back-again/.

But even when we know that 3 to 5% of people contribute to approximately 30% of the additional momentum[89] that we gain from cross functional efforts in project work, increased discretionary effort is not always a direct win. It can also lead to trouble.

Darker side of discretionary effort

Consider the tale of the business with an ancient website built on the wrong technology and wanted to replace it with the newest technology to give them a boost. The vision was that e-commerce could become a large part of their future business. One of the challenges they needed to overcome was that they had no one in the organisation to work on a new site while the existing site was in operation. In a difficult situation, they decided to recruit for the role of e-commerce manager before they had the new website live.

So, that person's job, for a time, was to work on the project. Once the project went live, their job would shift to managing the website and the team of people who were working on it. This was a smart move! By doing this they allowed for the continuity of knowledge and ensured that the project had at least one dedicated person on it all the time.

The difficulty came, however, when the website went live. The e-commerce manager moved into their new role of managing the website, but continued project effort was also required as there were multiple sites to go live. Things went a bit off the rails as the manager felt under pressure to continue to manage the project side of things at a full-time level, while also taking on the new full-time role of managing the website.

---

89   Cross. Collaborative Overload.

To handle the additional workload, the manager started taking shortcuts. They made promises that they could not keep. As their work suffered, their supervisors began to express concern about their workload. It was discussed, but tasks would get done in the nick of time, so the difficulties continued. Ultimately, the manager simply couldn't handle everything and began to covertly outsource their work to other people. Fortunately, it was uncovered, but the disruption to the team and business was extensive.

While we all want to do a good job and inspire team members to lift the bar, we also want to ensure that they're operating safely and within the guidelines of the business' expectations. Outsourcing your work to others creates problems regarding confidentiality and privacy, as well as not doing the work you were engaged to do. The discretionary effort of a team's people needs to be managed to avoid this sort of outcome.

Don't take discretionary effort for granted

What's important is to not take discretionary effort for granted. If we assume that people are doing the best that they can, then we won't push our existing employees to the point of breaking, which can often happen when they're tasked with both their regular full-time job and project work.

The reality is that you must involve the people who are on-ground experts at the business level in a change project. You must involve them because, to create buy-in for the change, the people who live there need to be making the decisions. They have the advantage of time spent in the business and a more accurate understanding of how business processes work, and they are more likely to foresee potential problems that will arise from making changes.

The horrible catch-22 is that the people who you want to do your project are often also critical from a day-to-day business point of view. Giving them double the work to do doesn't make it easy for them to function at their best. When you double the effort, you also double the bind that you're in.

It's a tricky balancing act.

Make sure if you're asking for more from people that you don't diminish the ask or sweep it aside. You know you're asking for more. So do they. If you can compensate the team in some way, then do. If you have the flexibility to give them time off or additional money, then consider that. Or ask, what might make this additional load easier for the team? Then do it.

Codifying purpose into your project

A small group of aligned people that understand the purpose of your project is vital to its success. Even more, it's inspiring to be part of an effort like this which can lead to further momentum. But that momentum will slip away unless this effort is codified and adopted by the wider organisation. If not, it remains a subculture.

Smart collaboration that leads to alignment that drives momentum involves us bringing those people who have deep expertise to solve broad problems that sit across a business. So, how do we build better collaborative muscles and align our project team to the project purpose?

Building alignment to purpose

Like most things in life and projects, aligning our project team to our organisation's purpose is not just about one or even two things. Focusing on only one or two things will not bring the results required. We need multiple elements working well to get to the successful outcomes we need.

Align the pipe (our people)

Much of our alignment effort must be focused on your people. Alignment of your people is the first step in my project approach, and there's some logic to that. The reason that I put alignment of people at the beginning of the working process is because often I see people keen to get into action. But if the actions are not aligned to the purpose, then duplication and confusion can take over. Project time is precious, so I want to ensure that the tasks you focus on are the ones that need doing and that wasted effort is minimised. And so focus first – and always – on aligning people with purpose.

One of my clients used to have a meeting that they referred to as the 'align the pipe' meeting. It's not a very glamorous name for a meeting, but it does give a very clear understanding of what the meeting is about. The intent of the session was to align the project to the purpose across all functional areas and ensure that everyone understood what was in progress and what it meant for them and their team. This client got very good results because they understood that building their vision was 99% alignment.

"Building a visionary company requires 1% vision and 99% alignment."

Jim Collins and Jerry Porer

When you're looking to 'align the pipe', you're looking to clarify how the project aligns with your business strategy. Where do those who are paying for and sponsoring the project see it delivering value? How does this line up with the business strategy?

Sometimes we work on projects that will be enablers for growth, particularly where a business has reached the end of what they can get from their current systems and are starting to confront technology limitations. From this, we can usually extract one or more purposes of the project. To be sure that you've nailed down the purpose, ask different people across the business what the purpose is. They should be able to give similar answers about what it is that you're doing and why.

If you're not getting the same or similar answers, then there's more work to do to align the team and individuals with the purpose of the project. More 'align the pipe' meetings might be needed, or more work with individual teams or people to ensure that everyone is clearly focused on the purpose of the project from the start.

Align the layers (the organisation)

In larger businesses, there are often multiple layers of alignment needed. We work from the action level of the business through the middle layers of team members, to executive and leadership and sometimes even boards. You need to think across the organisation and consider different functional teams and how they align with the projects. Functional teams want to understand their contributions to a project, as well as how it will touch their part of the business (if it does) or any existing processes.

You'll also need to create alignment with the partners who are working on the project. Whether they're the software vendors, infrastructure providers, consultants or other experts who are assisting you to set up your system, you must make sure that they're also clear about the purpose and scope of the project. Part of your alignment effort must be to provide support where it's needed across the entire organisation.

Align the tools (the operations)

The final piece of alignment is how you set up the tools. These include the ways of working, the software and hardware systems and overall operations for the project. If it's feasible, it's always a good idea to take some time to consider what these tools and systems might look like once the project is complete and embedded into ongoing business operations.

Making sure they're aligned with and supportive of your project and its integration is only one part of the thinking. The second part is making sure the ongoing systems and tools remain aligned with the overall purpose of the organisation, keeping in mind how this might change due to the changes brought on by the project itself.

Maintaining alignment with growth

Many (most!) projects that I've worked on have been part of an overall growth strategy. But growth comes with its own challenges in terms of maintaining alignment. As an organisation gets larger, you will need to put more effort into the work of keeping everybody aligned. You will need to be flexible and attuned to where your teams are, and how they view the purpose of the project. This will change – or be lost – over time and as new people and stakeholders are brought on board.

Part of your alignment strategy should include the constant review of your purpose, your teams and your people.

Building your purposeful project team

Building the right team for your project is arguably the most important step in ensuring alignment with your purpose. From the very first project that I worked on it was clear to me that the right team is an extraordinarily important part of successful project delivery.

The first ERP project I worked on was a Y2K project in the late 1990s. At the time it felt of critical importance to us all. I was a subject matter expert who had recently joined the company (so not really an expert at all). I expect that I ended up on the project team because they thought I might challenge existing current processes and be open to how the new system worked.

They were right, I suppose, because this turned out to be just my type of work. I had a great group of people to work with and it was the type of challenge I enjoy – learning a new system, figuring out ways of working and dedicating time to something that's of strategic importance. The project was a success, and I felt that I'd found a place to spend my working life.

I didn't know it then, but it turns out this project was very carefully set up for success (there had been multiple previous failed attempts), and this started with precise team selection. A cross functional team of people were seconded to the project. Everyone brought different skills and experience to the table. The project manager and testing manager were highly experienced and supported the project team fully. They expected (and allowed) the rest of the team to make decisions and encouraged us to check with the people in our teams first. Challenges were met and managed including, when part way through the project, one person resigned and the remainder of the team managed to pick up the extra work relatively quickly (maybe someone had foreseen that the resignation was on the cards?).

The combination of skills and attitude in the project team meant that we were able to get the job done successfully. It was the right people on the right team.

Mindset over skill set

When you're designing your own project team it's important to understand that it's not just a matter of skillset. It's a matter of attitude as well. Emotional intelligence or EQ (the ability to understand, use and manage your own emotions in positive ways) has had quite a lot of attention in recent years, but research is divided about its benefits and usefulness.

Adam Grant, in particular, says, 'Emotional intelligence is important, but the unbridled enthusiasm has obscured a dark side. New evidence shows that when people hone their emotional skills, they become better at manipulating others. When you're good at controlling your own emotions, you can disguise your true feelings. When you know what others are feeling, you can tug at their heartstrings and motivate them to act against their own best interests.'[90]

---

90   Grant, A. (8 October 2015). 'The Dark Side of Emotional Intelligence.' *Medium*. https://medium.com/@AdamMGrant/the-dark-side-of-emotional-intelligence-fda18dd53da4#:~:text=Emotional%20intelligence%20is%20important%2C%20but,can%20disguise%20your%20true%20feelings.

The most sensible position to me, however, seems that EQ is situational in that its effectiveness and application can vary greatly depending on the specific context or environment. However I've found that in most projects, EQ – and the mindset that delivers EQ – can be very important.

Project work requires teams to come together to form new teams to work towards a specific outcome. At the start of World War II, the then US president selected General William 'Wild Bill' Donovan to establish the country's first foreign intelligence service, named the Office of Strategic Services or OSS. Donovan had a novel idea of how to get the best staff. Instead of finding people to fit a preconceived plan, he hired the best that he could find and shaped the missions around them.

With talents as diverse as playwright Robert Sherwood and future celebrity chef Julia Child, Donovan created an agency that helped to score important victories for the Allied cause very soon after being formed. They were able to get the work started and their desired outcomes were reached in quick time.

Of course, not every business leader has such diversity, depth of experience and talent available as Wild Bill did, so more pragmatic choices may be needed. But it's helpful to think of this approach when you're forming your team and striving to get the most talented people on your team as possible will certainly benefit the project as a whole.

Once you have your team in place, it's time to start investing in them. You need to make sure they understand their roles and responsibilities, their relationships with each other as well as with partners and stakeholders, that they're given the opportunities and tools to complete their jobs well and that they're always treated with respect and consideration.

> "A good team makes the work go smoother (faster and better). Investing time and energy into developing that team means treating people with respect as a baseline."[91]

> Christine Porath

Let's pretend we're logical

A specialty retailer my team worked with on the sale of a division had an ERP project going live at the same time. Because of my position I had a front row seat as they went live with the ERP and the subsequent impact that unfolded.

The impact was intense.

They were not ready to go but the executive sponsor of the project used her position to push the system live anyway. The planning and allocation teams were only able to get data at very macro or micro levels and had trouble sifting through it to properly build the inventory as Christmas closed in. The quality control processes had shifted in the warehouse. They went from lax to stringent and the warehouse team struggled to receipt items into being available to pick. Teams in store had extreme data problems and no clarity of delivery expectations. Large deliveries

---

91 Porath, C. (2107). *Mastering Civility: A Manifesto for the Workplace.* Grand Central Publishing. Porath's study surveyed over 20,000 employees globally and found that employees who felt respected by their leaders reported:
56% better health and well-being, 89% greater enjoyment and satisfaction, 92% greater focus and prioritisation, 26% more meaning and significance, and 55% more engagement. Compelling statistics in a tide of what feels like increasing disinterest, dissatisfaction and disengagement.

were appearing on the busiest days and customers were unable to shop as team members tried to unpack boxes in the aisles. The business fell short of their Christmas trade targets by over 25% and store teams were overrun with cranky customers who were trying to buy gifts but could not get served.

In this example, the business came incredibly close to failing completely.

Martyn Newman, author of *Emotional Capitalists*, talks of the fundamental emotion that drives decision making.[92] We're all subject to our stated and conscious emotions, and the less aware we are of these emotions the less likely we are to make balanced choices. This applies to our teams as well, and to their own EQ.

One of my personal heroes, Douglas Adams, English author, humourist and screenwriter, best known for *The Hitchhiker's Guide to the Galaxy* book series, describes the idea of 'pre-setting' the decision outcome you're looking for and then building the logic around it. One of his characters, Gordon, invented some ingenious software:

> *Well, Gordon's great insight was to design a program which allowed you to specify in advance what decision you wished it to reach, and only then to give it all the facts. The program's task, which it was able to accomplish with consummate ease, was simply to construct a plausible series of logical-sounding steps to connect the premises with the conclusion.*[93]

Adams' great talent is to see human fallibility and to find a way to share and talk about it with humour. In amongst the irony and gentle mockery, there's a strong resonance between how project timelines and go live

---

92   Newman, M. (2104). *Emotional Capitalists: The Ultimate Guide to Developing Emotional Intelligence for Leaders*. RocheMartin.

93   Adams, Douglas. (1998). *Dirk Gently's Holistic Detective Agency* Pocket Books.

targets are often constructed. Rather than evaluating the work to be done and the quality of the outcome we're looking for, we have a decision to go live passed to us and then need to construct a 'way of getting there' in reverse.

The logical mind has, for a great deal of time, had greater perceived value than the emotional. It's not unusual to spend a lot of time and energy trying to make ourselves seem logical when a lot of what we do comes from that first emotional reaction. Recent research has shown that emotions play a crucial role in decision making. According to the research of neuroscientist Antonio Damasio,[94] people with damage to the part of the brain responsible for emotions often struggle to make decisions (even simple ones). This suggests that emotions are integral to the decision-making process.

Emotions can serve as a quick, intuitive response that helps us navigate complex situations rapidly.[95] They can also provide valuable information about our preferences and values, which logical analysis alone might not capture.

Your non-human team members

When it comes to building the right team, you don't always need to be limited to your living and breathing colleagues. Potential non-human

> When it comes to building the right team, you don't always need to be limited to your living and breathing colleagues.

---

94   Emotion and Decision. Changing Minds. http://changingminds.org/explanations/emotions/emotion_decision.htm.

95   Gladwell, M & Fox, B. (2005). Blink: The Power of Thinking Without Thinking. Back Bay Books.

team members might be just what you need to fill the gaps in your project team.

In fact, you're probably already doing this. The software you're implementing might be seen as a valued team member – one that you and your team can learn from and get to know (rather than be an imposed threat or inconvenience). Nadjia Yousif, expert in change within technology systems, organisational structures and digital customer experiences, made an entertaining comparison of onboarding a new team member and starting to use new software in a TED Talk.[96] It's a fun (and potentially insightful way) to think about potential team members.

Ask yourself, who or what else might be the right fit for your team? Would you consider adding AI 'team members' to your workforce? A more hybrid way of working doesn't just mean joining from whatever location. Today, hybrid ways of working also mean people and machines riffing and developing ideas together, for example, where AI and humans worked together to solve previously unsolved math problems.[97]

However you think the composition of your internal team will be, making space to consider some other options can open up new possibilities. The future certainly embraces alternate ways of thinking about the team, who is on it and how we engage with the software and machine intelligence aspects of our work.

---

96 Yousif, N. (October 2018). 'Why you should treat the tech you use at work like a colleague.' [Video]. Ted Conferences. https://www.ted.com/talks/nadjia_yousif_why_you_should_treat_the_tech_you_use_at_work_like_a_colleague.

97 Castlevecchi, D. (21 December 2023). 'AI Beats Humans on Unsolved Math Problem.' *Scientific American*. https://www.scientificamerican.com/article/ai-beats-humans-on-unsolved-math-problem/.

Building purpose into other players

Again, in larger businesses, there are often multiple layers of alignment needed and that's because there are a lot of additional players in the project. This includes partners, suppliers, experts and even customers. Your alignment effort must include making sure that they're also clear about the purpose and scope of the project.

Partners are part of the team too

Some time ago (admittedly over a drink), I overheard a software provider ask, 'What if we selected the people we want to work with first, and then figured out the plan and the system?' In a way, this is a mirror of the previously mentioned 'Wild Bill' approach of recruiting the talent and allowing those talents to shape the project.

Despite the innovative thought, this approach has not been used on a single project that I've worked on. Instead, they find the plan and the system, and then bring in the team to manage that plan and system. And often that means partners.

Typically, when businesses go about solving large technology problems, they're also working to keep their business functioning well. It's rare to be able to second an entire project team like in my first project experience. Asking for help doesn't mean there's anything wrong with your business.

All the businesses I work with are experts. They are experts at running successful businesses that serve their customers. They are experts in developing practices and processes that have got them to where they are today. They are experts in their market and market competition. They are experts on their customers' pain points. They are also often experts on what needs to improve to keep pace with customers. However, they are <u>not</u> all experts at the various elements needed to *deliver* a project. And that's why almost all successful projects need aligned partners.

Getting the right help means embracing complementary skills

Just like the adage 'opposites attract', partners that complement your skills can be an excellent way to build out the skillsets you need to successfully deliver your project. If you have great technical skills, then maybe you need a partner who brings amazing creative ideas. If your core systems cannot currently be replaced, then maybe the right partner for you is one who can complete integration work that is lightly coupled to existing systems and reduce rewrites later. If you're dealing with basic connectivity challenges, then perhaps your need is for a partner who can set up the infrastructure for you and stabilise the connections.

Understanding the strengths of your own team will help you to know who is going to bring the skills that complement those strengths to the table and make your project team more well-rounded. Partner skills are the most important of all the attributes that you're assessing.

It's worth mentioning that getting a partner of a complementary size is also helpful. This means partners who are the 'right size' to work with your business and who can grow and develop and continue to evolve with your business.

This is not to imply that you can't work with different sized organisations. This happens all the time and the variety these kinds of partnerships can bring is highly enriching. So it's worth considering and maybe getting curious about the plans of your partners.

Cultural compatibility

Each team and organisation has its own habits, rituals and systems that support the ways in which it works. When assessing your future partners, a sense check on cultural compatibility is another way to ensure that you can embrace a shared purpose, align your goals and create a long-term relationship that is set up for success. If you can ensure that your project partners are in alignment, working together will be smoother and easier.

To check your alignment to purpose, think about your attitudes to service, your focus on quality, your speed of response and your sense of ownership. While these things are not as tangible as cost and time, they absolutely do contribute to the successful delivery of your project because they relate to your ability to fully come into alignment.

And don't forget your stakeholders

'Stakeholders' is one of those project words that can sound a bit dehumanising. It connotes a nameless, faceless group of people that are not seen to add value to a project, but instead, at their most innocuous, competing desires, and at their most insidious, roadblocks and layers of bureaucracy. But stakeholders *are* a part of every project, and in order to promote real alignment, care should be taken to provide them with the opportunity to understand and embrace the purpose of the project as well.

Stakeholders are, essentially, people who are or may be interested in or impacted by the project that you're embarking on. They can exist both inside your business and as part of the value chain of your business. Suppliers are often stakeholders. So too are customers. It's unlikely you'll be having a one-on-one with every stakeholder, nor will you even meet them all. So building in alignment with purpose isn't a straightforward exercise.

To do so, you should be thinking about the impact of the project from the stakeholders point of view, ensuring that the lines of communication are open and operating both ways and creating a purpose that keeps the stakeholders in mind. This will assist you to build rapport with your stakeholders, even if they are not in the room or your organisation.

Foundation roles within your team

No matter the size of your project there are four foundational roles that are essential within your team. Like the four wheels on a car, they need to be pumped to the right level and all aligned in the same direction to work at their best.

1. **Vision makers/sponsors** are people who want to see the project succeed.

   They take on financial decisions and have the authority to approve expenses, assist with procuring any additional funds, if needed, and keep executive focus.

2. **Technical experts**, or subject matter experts, are people who know how the systems work.

   They have the right technical skills and ability to advise on the configuration or development of the system, and guide, based on expertise, on the match of system to the business process.

3. **Business experts** are those who will be using the system on a daily basis.

   These people have insight into how the business process works right now and know what needs to be done day-to-day. These are people who've got the right knowledge to be able to contribute to the project in the form of business process and improvements. They are the most impacted group in that they will inherit the outcome of the project.

4. **Project managers** are people who keep everyone heading in the same direction.

   These people co-ordinate and document the project's tasks, facilitate decision making, monitor the timeline, manage risks and mitigation strategies and stay focused on the goals of the project, to bring the project to fruition.

When you start preparing project teams and selecting (or negotiating for) people to contribute to the effort of a project, choosing the right combination of people from across the business and project partners makes all the difference. Each project has the need for a different blend of skills. Balancing that blend is the job of the project manager and sponsor.

Aligning your project systems

The final piece of the puzzle is aligning your project systems, tools and ways of working with your organisation's purpose. If you're trying to do something big across multiple partners, then set some rules of engagement or ways of working that feel complementary to your overall purpose in making the change. This ensures that everyone doing the doing is across them, understands your purpose and systems, and has access to any tools required.

In agile practice the first sprint is often a 'setting up' sprint where the teams that will work together establish the rhythm of the project. This includes where documentation will be kept, how decisions will be made, meeting cadences, participation and development tools, environment set up, connectivity and access.

A guiding principle to keep in mind as the owner of the project work is that you will need to refer back to these documents at some later date. Any future changes (and there will be some) will need documentation created as part of the project. Because of that it's a good idea to ensure that new systems are set up close to existing processes, storage or environment so that it's easy to find information and help when needed. The principle of storing documents where they will be used is a good principle to think about here.

Systems are the producers

Systems, of course, are not the fun or sexy part of business. I think of the systems part of a business as being a little bit like the stage manager or producer on a Broadway show. They do a lot of the hard work, coordinating, organising and making sure that everyone is working well together but it's not their name in lights. They're backstage. They're not the headline act. And they're not (usually) the people that draw in the crowd.

But while systems and back-end processes will likely never be the front face of your brand or the name over your door, your systems power the backend, and how well you are able to use systems and processes to your advantage can make a huge difference to the people who work for you, and to the suppliers and providers that you partner with. It will make a difference to the front facing and follow up customer teams, and that has a flow on impact to your customers.

As Richard Branson has said,

> *"If you look after your staff, they'll look after your customers. It's that simple."*

Systems and processes are the support structure that keeps teams working effectively or not. The right collaborative tools allow teams access to data without oversharing or compromising security. Though there's a natural tension between access to data and compliance that requires IT teams to develop the skills and relationships with businesspeople (and HR) for timely and complete onboarding and offboarding of information and people. So too, people across functions must connect systems with routines that enable cross sharing of information and perspectives.

This is transparency. When you have alignment in your systems, it supports transparency between your cross-functional teams which can then lead to exponential results in your projects. And it also builds in efficiencies and reduces wasted efforts. If you find that you don't have transparency in your project, it's likely that you're not as aligned as you think.

Providing systems and support structures that allow your staff to look after your customers can make a big difference to where your team uses their focus and energy. Do they spend the time chasing their tails trying to make sense of mismatching data or do they look after your customers? Only one of these things is a potential repeat purchaser.

Sharing information, systems, tools and ways of working allows your wider team – including contractors, vendors and your internal team – to align both together and with your overall purpose. As things change over time, check back in to ensure that the documentation covers those changes, and that everyone knows the ways of working for the project, the project's implementation and the post change future.

Challenges to building out your 'perfect' aligned project

Of course, there is no perfectly aligned project. But if you can get your projects aligned to strategy, studies show that you're 57% more likely to deliver benefits to the business, 50% more likely to finish on time and 45% more likely to stay on budget.[98] Even partial alignment can significantly improve project outcomes.[99] We all know, however, that even the best laid plans (or projects!) can face challenges. And just as alignment revolves around people, your challenges often do as well.

1. There's no perfect team

While the goal is to get the 'perfect' suite of team members who are aligned with your organisation's purpose, and focused on working hard, delivering value and building true collaboration, most of the time, this simply won't happen. For one thing, you won't always get to choose every member of your project team. You may inherit project participants – in fact, for us, this happens more often than not.

If you find yourself in this situation, a skills gap analysis is helpful so you can build out an inherited team with additional skills. When you're coming into a team that's already formed, start by getting a sense of how the team is operating. This will allow you to figure out where the

---

98   Springer, A. (9 October 2022). 'The importance of strategic alignment in project management.' Atlassian Community. https://community.atlassian.com/t5/Jira-articles/The-importance-of-strategic-alignment-in-project-management/ba-p/2157556.

99   Springer. The importance of strategic alignment in project management.

problems are and what skills gaps need plugging. Then take a look at who your ideal team member would be to plug that gap. Remember, this team member might actually be non-human!

2. Your team will be inexperienced

Most of the time I find myself helping businesses that don't 'do' projects all the time. That's because for most organisations, projects are naturally outside the scope of normal business activities. So, the people who have been moved into a project role may have no idea what's expected of them or how to execute on those expectations. This lack of project experience can cause friction and delays in all stages and can cause an aligned team to fall out of alignment, not from any resistance or a lack of purpose, but simply from inexperience.

Here clarity of what's expected of each role is helpful. This includes the role, the associated responsibilities *and* the required relationships. Begin by defining what each person's role is and what they are responsible for at the outset. Getting clarity about what's expected and who is required to do what makes it easier for people to plan their own work and contribute when and where they're most needed. Then you need to align each person's relationships for the most effective collaboration.

Roles: A team member's everyday role is not the same as their project role. It's the responsibility of the project manager to ensure that each team member's role is clearly defined, including their responsibilities and the key tasks they will be performing.

Responsibilities: Clear responsibilities help ensure that tasks are completed on time and to the required standard. Project teams should know who is responsible for specific tasks and the impact of responsibilities being unclear or missed.

Relationships: Building positive relationships between team members is essential for effective collaboration. There are a lot of moving parts in a large-scale change project and having multiple people communicating with one vendor (for example) can result in confusion and the wasting of time and energy as people try to clarify what's really meant.

On the other hand, teams who agree how team members will communicate with each other (and with vendors!) and how they will manage conflicts or issues that may arise during the project are better prepared for bumps along the road when they occur.

Our experience teaches us that if we can foster positive working relationships between team members, contractors and vendors without needing to be in the middle of every conversation, often these people figure out solutions and share information with one another that better serves the project objectives.

3. There's a lack of understanding about infrastructure and systems

Businesses who have not done a lot of projects will often have either a very lean IT department or no IT specialists in their business. They may have outsourced tasks that focus primarily on infrastructure and hardware set up and 'keeping the lights on'. It's not unusual for a business of this structure to have a low understanding of infrastructure and systems set up.

Businesses that are more experienced and evolved in projects and technology will often have a process or a set of criteria that needs to be approved under various scenarios. For example, when it comes to approving new vendors, they would have an onboarding process and active and clear vendor management and ways of working, as well as clear reporting cadence and defined service levels.

Your business structure will typically require a strong panel of internal experts who understand the relationship, have a clear understanding of the roadmap and the purpose to which it's aligned and can hold others to account.

4. Roles and responsibilities will change

Roles and responsibilities will change over the life of your project (of any project!). So they should be revisited, reassessed and reaffirmed at key points throughout the project life cycle. The roles required at the beginning of a new project are not the same as those required for a project that's been 'done before'. And a project that has custom new development is not the same as one that requires configuration.

Starting the project strong with clear expectations of the role (value) that each team member is bringing to the table is a foundational element. Resetting expectations and re-aligning at points through the project lifecycle sets your team up to avoid the missteps of misconstrued roles.

When should we reconsider roles and responsibilities? Before user testing commences is a good time to reset roles and responsibilities. This phase of the project often involves a wider group of people, and it's a good time to confirm and reset who is doing what. Operationalising is the way we describe the 'handing over' of the project work to business teams.

The project team would typically engage more deeply in training, testing and handover activities to 'stick' the landing of the project. Revisiting roles, responsibilities and relationships during these phases of a project gives us a natural break point where we can re-examine what's needed and ensure that everyone is aligned on project objectives.

True alignment builds vital momentum

The alignment of your people and systems to your overall purpose contributes to a consistency and rhythm that will create momentum. This momentum drives your project forward, creating opportunities for high performance and, therefore, a successful change project.

Without alignment, you're going to face far more friction, delays, miscommunications, mistakes and challenges. You can think of each of these things as dragging behind you as you try to move the project towards the finish line, slowing you down each step of the way.

On the other hand, alignment builds a consistent rhythm that sees you moving towards the finish line gathering speed as you go.

But your job isn't done. As you get into the nuts and bolts of your project, you will find that transparency and communication – while always important – take on a larger part of your mindset.

Transparency

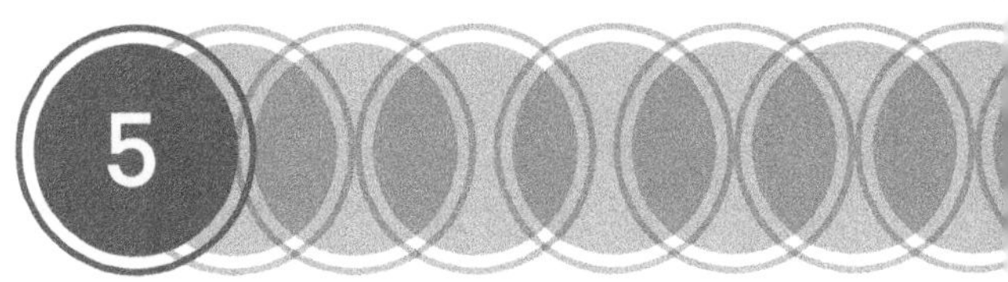

As we explored in the last chapter, alignment is all about shared purpose and strategic focus. These are the keys to driving momentum in any change project. But they aren't the only thing that matters. You cannot have a truly high-performing team – one that adopts a shared purpose and works collaboratively to achieve change that aligns with that purpose – without transparency.

If alignment sets the direction, transparency ensures the clarity and coherence of the journey. It is the lens through which we observe, understand and guide the intricate processes that propels our projects forward. And without a clear lens, we simply can't see what's going on.

In every successful project, transparency supports collaboration and trust among team members. But without it, even the most aligned and well-intentioned teams can falter.

In this chapter, we'll explore the mechanisms and tools that foster transparency, and how they can be harnessed to build stronger, more high performing and aligned teams. Through transparency, we transform the abstract concepts of strategy and alignment into actionable steps that everyone can follow. This ensures that your team is moving as a whole toward your common goal.

Transparency is the lens to see and guide our projects

Researchers have frequently demonstrated that greater transparency — whether amongst countries or companies — leads to greater credibility and thus value. For example, the International Monetary Fund (IMF) concluded in a 2005 research paper that countries with more transparent fiscal practices have more credibility in the market, better fiscal discipline, and less corruption.[100]

The Global Accountability Project ran for a decade and sought to bring greater levels of transparency and accountability to large and influential inter-governmental organisations, multinational corporations and international organisations, with the aim of enhancing their accountability.[101] The project, with the aim of increasing transparency globally, did focus on increasing it within its own ranks first. It includes transparency in its framework, defining it as the 'provision of accessible and timely information to stakeholders and the opening up of organisational procedures, structures and processes to their assessment.'[102]

100 Hameed, F. (2005). *Fiscal Transparency and Economic Outcomes*. IMF Working Paper; WP/05/225. International Monetary Fund. https://www.imf.org/external/pubs/ft/wp/2005/wp05225.pdf.

101 Global Accountability. One World Trust. https://www.oneworldtrust.org/accountability.html.

102 Blagescu, M, de Las Casas, L & Lloyd, R. (2005). *Pathways to Accountability: A short guide to the GAP Framework*. One World Trust. https://acfid.asn.au/sites/site.acfid/files/resource_document/pathways_to_accountabilityl.pdf.

When it comes to creating successful change projects, as the IMF knows, transparency is not just about visibility. It's about creating an environment where information flows appropriately, where everyone knows their role, where expectations are clearly defined and where purpose is your North Star.

Transparency is about endowing every single person on the project with clarity, understanding and a clear path forward to achieving your shared purpose. It's about making sure that every team member can see the road ahead, understand the obstacles and contribute effectively to the project's success.

The problem with opacity

When we don't have transparency in our projects, we're left with the opposite – opacity.

So often, the systems that we're working on improving are held together with what I describe as goodwill and bandaids. Whilst the goodwill part of this may have a lot of positives associated with it, it can also mask bottlenecks and ineffective working processes. It's the lack of transparency around data and targets that mean we're reliant on the goodwill to start with. When we work with clients who have focused on goodwill without data, we want to preserve the relationship and bring an additional lens that's more empirical to the table as a complement.

We need to remember that the project's purpose should align to our strategic gains – in other words, in some way it should uplift and improve the business. This means that the systems we use and tools that support those systems need to have some rigour and controls around them.

But too often we have band aids on top of band aids, which makes it difficult to see the true 'injuries' in our systems. And these bandaids work exactly as they sound – they stem the flow of blood, but they don't solve the underlying problem.

The HIH example

HIH Insurance was Australia's second largest insurance company prior to 2001, when it collapsed in a truly spectacular fashion. In fact, it's considered to be the largest corporate collapse in Australia's history, with experts estimating that its total losses were up to $5.3 billion.

So what happened to HIH? Well many things, but one contributing factor was likely a lack of transparency. Like many companies, it grew through acquisition. And each additional company that it acquired, brought with it its own accounting system. So by 2001 HIH had business divisions running seven different accounting systems.[103] These multiple systems led to discrepancies and difficulties in consolidating financial data, increased the risk of errors (and actual errors) and then made it harder to detect financial problems in a timely way. For HIH, mismanagement and poor corporate governance were already issues, so the additional complexity added by multiple accounting systems exacerbated these problems. There was a complete lack of transparency which hindered effective decision-making.

For HIH, trying to interpret and understand data across different systems made it incredibly difficult to see what the business was doing as a whole. There was simply no visibility. Was this a contributing factor to its downfall? Seems likely.

---

103 The Treasury. (19 June 2015). 'Aftermath of the HIH collapse.' Australian Government. https://treasury.gov.au/publication/economic-roundup-issue-1-2015/economic-roundup-issue-1/the-hih-claims-support-scheme/3-aftermath-of-the-hih-collapse.

A lack of transparency can lead to a raft of problems including (ultimately) complete organisational failure. Or in our case, project failure. But total failure isn't always the result – other less dramatic, but still difficult challenges can arise when the people on your team don't have real visibility.

1. Challenging relationships (fear of the unknown)

The psychological term for fear of the unknown is 'xenophobia'. It is the tendency to be afraid of something you have no information about on any level.[104] Without transparency in our projects, there is a lot that is unknown. And researchers have found that this can also lead to a habit of catastrophising, which is imagining worst case scenarios. When our team is afraid of what they don't know, and begins to catastrophise, they lose their ability to see the big picture, they become misaligned and this type of thinking gets in the way of an accurate view of reality.[105]

'Trust is the best tool for driving out fear,' says Pixar co-founder Ed Catmull[106] and building in transparency can improve trust. People understand what their roles are and the expectations they're meant to deliver on. They also have the data and information they need to meet those expectations well.

We know that relationships are key to a high performing and collaborative team. But team members who feel ignorant about or kept out of the loop in the business are not going to have trust in their

104 Stanborough, R. (23 July 2020). 'Understanding and Overcoming Fear of the Unknown.' healthline. https://www.healthline.com/health/understanding-and-overcoming-fear-of-the-unknown.
105 Stanborough. Understanding and Overcoming Fear of the Unknown.
106 Popova, M. 'Pixar Cofounder Ed Catmull on Failure and Why Fostering a Fearless Culture Is the Key to Groundbreaking.' *The Marginalian*. https://www.themarginalian.org/2014/05/02/creativity-inc-ed-catmull-book/.

colleagues, partners or project leads.[107] Worse, a lack of transparency can foster an 'us versus them' mentality which undermines collaboration and safety within the workplace.

People that are in this situation don't want to come to their project leads or managers to discuss what's going on.[108] They may simply continue to work in the only way they understand, becoming more and more resistant to change (and we've seen the problems with a resistant team) or they may just quit, leaving a gap in the project's skillset.

On the other hand, relationships are built up when there is a transparent working environment. This is where leaders and managers are seen to embrace open and honest communication, roles and responsibilities are clearly understood and the tools are in place to help individuals do their jobs well. In this situation, people have less reason to feel distrustful of those they're working with and are far more open to collaboration.

2. Inability to find balance

Various fields, including governance, politics, software design and business have experimented with the concept of 'radical transparency'.[109] Radical transparency emerged as a response to the soaring availability and dissemination of information in the digital age

---

107 Campbell, M. (21 May 2021). '3 Major Challenges in Change Management; and How to Tackle Them.' Prosci. https://www.proscisingapore.sg/blog/3-major-challenges-in-change-management-and-how-to-tackle-them.

108 'How a Lack of Transparency Can Cost Your Organization. coAmplifi. https://coamplifi.com/blog/how-a-lack-of-transparency-can-cost-your-organization/.

109 Hammett, R. (23 May 2018). '3 Steps Ray Dalio Uses Radical Transparency to Build a Billion-Dollar Company.' Inc. Australia. https://www.inc-aus.com/gene-hammett/3-steps-ray-dalio-uses-radical-transparency-to-build-a-billion-dollar-company.html; Tim, D. (3 May 2022). 'Let the sunshine in: The pitfalls of radical transparency.' Ethics.org. https://ethics.org.au/the-pitfalls-of-radical-transparency/.

and is believed to be able to help rebuild the 'increasingly strained' trust in institutions, government and business.

When radical transparency is directed towards the public it can serve to rebuild some of the trust that has been undermined and lost. Angela Knox, Associate Professor of Work and Organisation and Academic Director (Professional Development) from the University of Sydney, says that radical transparency is probably overstated as 'the panacea for organisations – something that's going to solve all of our problems.'[110] She believes instead that, 'in reality, it could very easily breed a culture of fear and intimidation.'[111]

So, instead of radical transparency, we're looking to find the right balance. Too little transparency and your team operates in the dark. This leads to misalignment, mistrust and mistakes. But too much and you risk overwhelming people or exposing sensitive information. The goal is to provide transparency with balance. Enough clarity so that everyone understands your project's goals and their own roles within the project.

When we're talking about balance, we're not speaking about the experiments cited at Zappos, where they tried an ambitious form of

> When radical transparency is directed towards the public it can serve to rebuild some of the trust that has been undermined and lost.

---

110 Stapleton, D. (18 May 2021). 'Radical transparency at work: clear cut or cut throat?' HRM. https://www.hrmonline.com.au/section/strategic-hr/radical-transparency-work/.
111 Stapleton. Radical transparency at work.

self-management called Holacracy[112]. Under the Holacracy system, self-governing teams were supposed to work in circles without any formal decision maker. But this was a hard slog. And it simply didn't pay off,[113] in particular when companies took a closed, top down, dogmatic and mandatory approach (it did work better when companies such as Bol.com took an open, bottom up, pragmatic and voluntary approach, which embraced only some elements of Holacracy).[114] We're also not talking about transparency that puts poor performers up on boards for naming and shaming or exposes everybody's salary to the entire company.

When we're looking to create balanced transparency within our change projects, we need to remember that we often focus on solving the extremes – they're easier to recognise and make for better stories (hence why we focus on them here as well!). But typically that's not where we're coming from in change projects. Instead the real work lies in managing the nuances of transparency – ensuring that the right amount of information is shared at the right time, with the right people. This is how we foster trust and alignment without creating unnecessary complexity.

3. Losing focus on your purpose (misalignment and misdirection)

The purpose that's driving your change project is what guides your strategy and keeps you aligned and focused on the target. So losing focus on this undermines all these things – your strategy, your alignment, your success.

---

112 Bernstein, E et al. 'Beyond the Holacracy Hype.' Harvard Business Review. https://hbr.org/2016/07/beyond-the-holacracy-hype.

113 Bernstein. Beyond the Holacracy Hype.

114 Minnaer, J. (22 August 2020). 'Two Large-Scale Holacracy Experiments: Zappos.com vs. Bol.com.' Corporate Rebels. https://www.corporate-rebels.com/blog/zappos-versus-bol.

Without transparency, team members aren't able to stay informed about your organisation-wide goals. And when they aren't informed about your goals, they can't make decisions aligned with those goals. A lack of transparency can lead to misalignment between the project goals and the actions of team members. When employees do not have a clear understanding of the project's objectives and their roles within it, they may make decisions that are not aligned with the overall goals, leading to inefficiencies.

On an individual level people that don't have a clear view of the goals and purpose will become frustrated and resistant. They may check out, put in minimum effort or, in the worst case scenario, actively try to undermine the work that's being done.

The right amount of transparency allows people to see the purpose, the goals and the road that can lead to accomplishing those. When challenges pop up, and they inevitably will, your team will be able to step up and meet those challenges with their purpose firmly at the front of mind.

4. Lack of engagement from those that matter

The less transparency in a workplace, the lower rates of engagement. Effective internal communications motivate 85% of employees to become more engaged in the workplace. This isn't enough, of course, to have a high performing and collaborative team.[115] Transparency needs to go beyond just 'effective internal communications'. It needs to be clear and available at all times and for everyone on the team.

115   Knilans, G. (12 June 2018). 'Using Internal Communications to Enhance Business Growth'. Trade Press Services. https://www.tradepressservices.com/internal-communications/.

The repercussions of a disengaged team on a change project is enormous. It impacts productivity, increases absenteeism, leads to low quality work and even contributes to a higher team turnover creating skills gaps you just don't need.

Project sponsors play an essential role in ensuring transparency, and therefore engagement, are maintained throughout the lifecycle of a change project. That's because project sponsors act as the bridge between the project team and the broader organisation. They not only provide resources, support and direction to keep the project moving in the right direction. But they're often also responsible for the culture of transparency (or not!) that a team, organisation and project have.

Project sponsors have a responsibility to model transparency by being clear about project objectives, timelines and expectations. They also need to be open to feedback from the project team, encouraging open communication where discussion and information sharing is the standard approach.

When sponsors actively engage in transparent practices, they build trust and accountability. They empower project managers and team members. This builds in clarity around roles, responsibilities and decision-making processes, and helps prevent the confusion, inefficiencies and delays that can arise from opacity. Ultimately, the project sponsor's commitment to transparency strengthens team cohesion, and keeps everyone aligned with the project's goals in the long term.

5. Less input from those in the know

Transparency works both ways. When it comes to understanding what's really going on in a change project and in a business, leaders need to be able to tap into the knowledge of everyone on their team – everyone at every level. And to do that, leaders need to share the problems and challenges that arise during the life of the project and be prepared to listen to the information, insights and input from those that are in the know.

Open lines of communication ensure that leaders have the information from the people who are on the ground, doing the work, gathering the data. Everyone is in the know then, and when a team feels confident to present insights to others, the input from those various parties might deliver a better solution to a problem or a challenge facing the project. Mutual problem solving will benefit the entire organisation.

6. Project failure

Of course the biggest and most obvious outcome from a lack of transparency in your project is that it fails. This might seem overly dramatic, and of course there are usually other contributing factors when a project goes belly up, but a lack of transparency is a big one.

When you're making choices about which systems to replace and what technology to implement, it's important to understand what decisions you're actually making.

If you have a really old ERP system and you're building out additional systems around that ERP, you might want to consider reexamining whether or not the system should be replaced instead.

This happened with one of our clients who, in an effort to avoid spending money on their ERP during an e-commerce upgrade, ended up with more additional systems than they first expected. The e-commerce project platform of choice had been decided, chosen because it offered a marketing aspect to the platform. So it had both an e-commerce and a marketing element to it, and the project team set out to deliver this new, improved e-commerce experience. However, along the way, they discovered that they needed an integration layer. The interpretations of the modern e-commerce tool were not going to jive with the ancient ERP, so they added the integration layer. Somewhat further through the project, it came to light that they would also need modern warehouse management software. It turned out that their existing ERP warehouse management software couldn't handle the way the e-commerce flow worked. So, in the end, they had five new systems to implement across multiple countries rather than one robust ERP system.

The complexity and the effort involved in doing that could have been significantly reduced if they had instead considered replacing their ERP and making the logic in the warehouse work better for the new ERP. It's very easy to analyse this after the fact with the benefit of hindsight, but it's worth considering in the process of system review. It's hard to pause a project and change direction. Even more so when you've spent years trying to get the investment in e-commerce over the line to start with. So it's understandable why they made the choices that they did.

However, addressing the core issue of the very old ERP by simply replacing it would have meant less in terms of vendors and integrations and ended in a system far more appropriate for what they wanted to do. What looks like a saving at the start of a project can keep costing you for years after the implementation is complete.

How to build up transparency

Of course, it's one thing to say what transparency is, and to believe in its importance for your change project. It's another thing entirely to explain how to build it into your projects and business workings.

Let's start with the basics. As we mentioned above, one of the key factors in transparency is the search for balance.

To create the right balance, we're striving for a match between the level of transparency and responsibility. 'If client service is everyone's responsibility, then data on service levels should be available to all; but if decisions about which product lines to invest in and which ones to cut are the CEO's responsibility, they should have privileged access to the information needed to make those decisions.'[116]

To that end we usually end up with a project structure that has a few layers. We're trying to walk a balanced line between the need for confidentiality and guiding people with the right information so that we avoid the pitfalls that come when people feel like they have no visibility of what's going on. Depending on your culture and organisation and the size of the project you're working on you may experience these layers in different ways. In some businesses there are only two, and in some there may be four, but thinking about it in three layers gives us a place to start.

Inner sanctum

The inner sanctum are people who have carriage of contracts and details of budgets. They may also need access to employee information and to systems that enable decision making and guide the project to completion in a timely manner. These are the people ultimately responsible for the project success and usually include

> The inner sanctum are people who have carriage of contracts and details of budgets.

---

116 Birkinshaw, J & Cable, D. (1 February 2017). 'The dark side of transparency.' *McKinsey Quarterly*. https://www.mckinsey.com/capabilities/people-and-organizational-performance/our-insights/the-dark-side-of-transparency#/.

the project sponsor, the project manager and some key decision makers in the business.

Working party

The working party – those who are 'running the show' – must have what they need to do their project job, and enough so that they're not caught out by surprises coming out of left field. They've got the right amount of information to do the work that's ahead of them, and they've also got enough confidence and comfort to find out more if they feel that they need that to be more effective. In mature teams with emotionally attuned people they will often self select out of a conversation if they don't need to be there.

Impacted stakeholders

It's important to be transparent with stakeholders but they typically need less information. Since they're not making decisions or doing the work they're more likely to want to know 'when' and 'what' it means for them. It's feasible that you may have more than one stakeholder group across the existence of your project. Those who are barely impacted probably need a courtesy call before go live to ensure that they're aware. Stakeholders who are more impacted (like those who will need to use a new system) will need detailed training and communication plans prior to go live as well as follow up sessions and the opportunity to share feedback through the project.

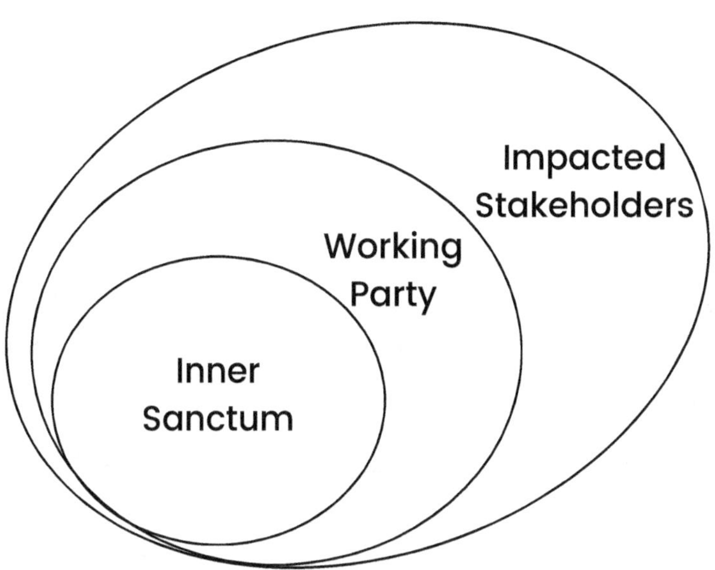

Shared information and systems

When it comes to transparency in action, it is all about creating shared information, access and systems that support our working teams. Tactically, transparency is a lot about the tools that support what it is that we're doing – quick and timely information exchange, clarity around when tasks are complete and when they need to be escalated for resolution. Visibility of concurrent activities, black out periods and the cadence of the business calendar all help to build up a picture that allows us to anticipate any moves around resourcing and potential conflicts.

The intent of creating transparent systems is to minimise inconsistencies and surprises, and foster the collaborative, trusting working environment that we're looking to build. It also has that additional capacity to keep us on track and hold us all accountable because everyone can see what's going on in real time. Platforms and systems that give visibility and access to all who are working on a project contribute to creating that transparency.

People and processes

The systems we create for project delivery should facilitate communication with clarity. The underlying assumption being that there is no need for secrets inside the project. But it's not all about the systems as we well know. People and processes also feed into what the systems are doing.

If the project strategy and alignment piece is sound then transparency is, to some extent, baked in. Clarity of purpose and what success looks like are guiding lights. And with the establishment of our team, who understands their purpose and goals, comes the establishment of roles, responsibilities and relationships, as well as communication and reporting channels all of which support transparency. They allow us to get ahead of or reroute any actions that are potentially off track.

Transparency among your people and processes also helps support your risk and issue management throughout the life of the project. The ability to see clearly helps you to ensure that the project team are proactively documenting risks as well as revisiting any risks they've identified to make sure the management plan is reducing or maintaining the risk level. Without this clarity, risks can appear and compound without the project team or leads even recognising them.

Automation

I think one of the other pieces that we can bring into this conversation is how we can automate tasks to build in more transparency. Automating processes within a team can significantly enhance transparency in a number of ways.

1. **Consistency and standardisation.** Automated tasks are performed consistently every time, and reducing variability means that each team member can have a clear and exact understanding of what is being done, when and how. Consistency leads to standardisation, which reduces misunderstandings and increases clarity.

2. **Real-time monitoring and tracking.** Many automated systems and processes have in-built tracking, monitoring and reporting features. That means that the team can have the same data, reported in a standard form, in real time.

3. **Accountability.** Automation can often create comprehensive logs and audit trails of every action taken within a system. This means that any team member can access the history of a task or process, see who was responsible for each action and understand the decision-making process. This level of access promotes accountability and ensures that everyone is on the same page.

4. **Reduction of human error.** Human error will always happen. But when it does it can lead to misunderstandings, miscommunications and even hidden mistakes. This affects transparency across the team and the project. By automating repetitive or complex tasks, the likelihood of errors is reduced, making the entire process more transparent.

5. **Clear workflow visibility.** Automation tools often include dashboards and visual management systems that display workflows in a clear, understandable format. This visibility allows team members to see where bottlenecks occur, how tasks are flowing through the system and where resources are being allocated. This results in team members being able to have a clearer picture of the entire process, from start to finish.

Clearer communication

I'm always a fan of encouraging direct and complete communication – so, straightforward ways of talking. There's no need for additional buzzwords or hysterics. Just explain where you're coming from as best you can.

Clear communication is kind communication (we'll explore this more later), but it's also transparent communication. It keeps everyone on the same page, providing them with all the information they need to continue working towards the end goals.

Transparency provides space for conflict and courage

Conflict is inherently dangerous. Most people, me included, shy away from conflict.

Most of the work of technology projects is with people at desks and screens. Not a lot of physical danger there.[117] However, research tells us that our brains experience no difference between physical and emotional (or psychological) pain.[118] The pain experienced from tearing a ligament in your knee and the pain experienced by social isolation or rejection is, for our brains, the same.

Putting ideas forward or speaking up in a group involves an element of risk, and so this requires some fortitude. Like most things, risk exists on a spectrum. Whether it's the temporary discomfort of looking foolish

------

117   Unless an invasion happens in the country where people you're working with are located. This happened with Ukraine and the physical danger that our vendor partner's team was in was very real.

118   Lieberman, M. (8 October 2013). *Social: Why Our Brains Are Wired to Connect*. Crown Pub.

(minor on the spectrum) or a 'I could lose my job' type of risk (major on the spectrum), it still requires an element of courage.

Projects need space for conflict and courage, because the first will certainly occur, even in the most well-managed projects, and the second will be needed to deal with the first. And transparency gives us the space for both.

Of course, the initial goal of transparency in a project is to forestall conflict. When roles, responsibilities and relationships are clearly defined, workflows are visible and accountability is the watchword of the entire team, and if all of this is supported by clear communication, many conflicts will be avoided. But not all. Conflicts are simply a part of the project landscape. But transparency helps even where conflicts are not avoided, because it creates a safe space built from trust and rapport (built in the first place by transparency!) where people can come manage the project conflicts.

Courage and fear

Brené Brown defines courage as 'the willingness to open up, be authentic, and be seen, even when you can't control the outcome. Courage involves facing uncertainty, emotional exposure and the potential for criticism or rejection.'[119]

The key point in the context of businesses undertaking projects, and the teams that deliver them, is that being courageous means facing uncertainty, potential criticism and rejection. Doing 'the right thing' if it goes against the prevailing view can be very dangerous. Not just in the moment but for the future of your career, mental health and earning potential.

---

119 Brown, B. (2021). *Atlas of the Heart: Mapping Meaningful Connection and the Language of Human Experience.* Random House.

If a risk, once taken, results in being shunned or derided then we experience a type of pain. It's this anticipation of potential pain and loss of social acceptance that is one of the things getting in the way of project teams doing their best work.

Creating safety is not enough

If there's no forum in which to share changing needs, develop ideas for how to address them and to align with different departments on how to meet the change, then nothing changes. Or worse, things change but in a chaotic, uncoordinated and potentially damaging way. To effectively implement a change requires multiple functional teams to be working to the same end goal. To lead this well you will need to create some structure that allows the team working on your project to exchange ideas easily – this is accomplished when you have a focus on transparency.

Lack of capacity

It's not just the fear of rejection that stops people from putting ideas forward. In businesses where team members do feel safe and the leaders are approachable and inclusive, we still see project activities getting stuck. Usually this is because they're not sure what to do. Maybe one or two team members have worked on a change project but that doesn't mean they know how to execute it themselves. Or, there is someone who has an idea of what to do, but they lack the capacity to get it done. Perhaps they have a job already and the project is 'extra'.

These businesses are usually very well meaning and have good working relationships. But they don't have a structure that supports the cross functional review of ideas or a forum in which to align and consider changes from multiple angles and make the decisions required to keep the project moving. This will be discovered if you have transparent workflows and accountability baked into your project, its people and processes.

No one works alone

You've heard the saying that 'no one is an island' – in projects we cannot work alone.

The whole point of a project is that it requires coordinated effort from different functional areas of a business. It needs those who are deeply knowledgeable about their areas to represent their own needs and consider the end-to-end process ensuring that their specialist body of knowledge has been considered as part of the change effort.

It requires those who can look ahead to the trends that are emerging and think about the future needs of their customers and stakeholders. The collective genius of the best teams is required to navigate change projects. But the collective genius must be shared, and that is through a focus on transparency.

How much transparency have you created?

Transparency is not merely a buzzword. In the right balance it's the lifeblood of successful change management. Project transparency really allows us to establish expectations and improve our focus.

> Transparency is not merely a buzzword. In the right balance it's the lifeblood of successful change management.

Without the right levels of transparency, teams are left navigating in the dark, vulnerable to miscommunication, misalignment and, ultimately, project failure. However, when transparency is prioritised and actively cultivated, it empowers individuals to contribute their best work, fosters a culture of open communication and creates a shared understanding that keeps everyone moving in the same direction.

Having access to all the information that you need is the easiest way to get a team moving with the momentum that you're looking for.

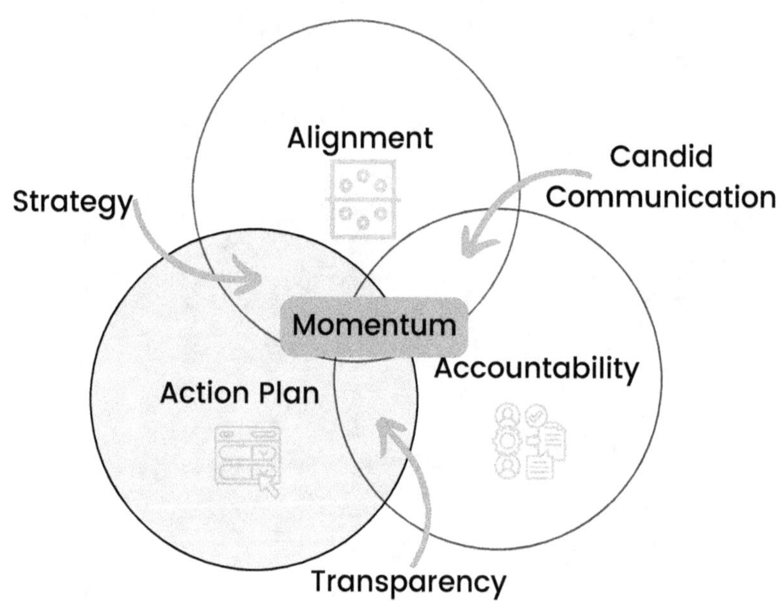
Alignment
Candid
Communication
Strategy
Momentum
Accountability
Action Plan
Transparency

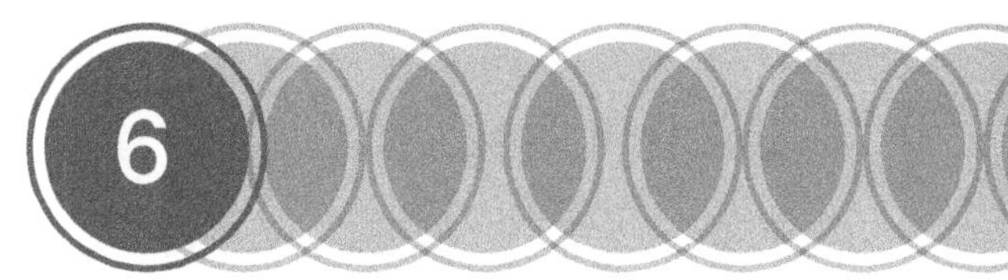

Action (Part 1)

In any change project, many assume the hard work ends once the software is selected and contracts signed. However, the real challenge often begins after this. Of course, if you're not prepared for this – or your team isn't – it can be disheartening, or downright demoralising. It's like reaching the summit of a hill only to discover another, steeper climb ahead. But this is the reality many businesses face as they move from software selection to implementation and finally to the critical phase of embedding the new system into daily operations.

Each of these phases presents unique challenges, and those challenges will require not just technical expertise but also strong leadership and team cohesion. In all change projects, understanding these phases and where you stand is crucial.

In this chapter, we'll explore the three big phases of software implementation and how to navigate them successfully so that your team not only reaches the next hill but strides up the trail.

3 big phases

A change project implementing new software typically has three main phases. The first big piece of work is **software selection**. The next big piece is the **software implementation**. Now many people think that once software implementation is done, they're done. But in actuality there's a third phase, sometimes the largest even, which is **learning how to use the software and realising it's benefits**.

PHASE 1: Software selection – and why you *must* choose

Maybe you're at the point where you KNOW you need a system change. Your first step will be to choose the software that meets your needs. The most significant of these is usually an integrated ERP (enterprise resource planning) change, which impacts the systems of your entire organisation. But whether you're replacing one large system or trying to plug a functional gap with something that connects systems better or fills a need that is not being met there is one absolute must.

You must choose

Choosing a system can be for the long haul, or it can be a stepping stone, knowing that you need to level up to be ready for something bigger or eliminate waste. Whether you're choosing tactically or strategically, it's important that the decision is made by someone in the business that will own and operate the systems. You can certainly engage an external party to guide you and help you assemble the information to make informed decisions – the decision is still being made by you. However, I strongly advise against getting an external party to make a recommendation (which is often just decision abdication in disguise) and then implement it for you.

Abdicating decision making sets you up for failure. It's a bit like seeing an outfit on somebody else, buying it and assuming it will look the same on you. Like body types, every business is unique and you need to choose the system(s) that will best suit you.

Some time ago I had an experience that highlights the importance of choosing your software for yourself. I was really delighted to get to work with this new business and their team. They were young and innovative, they had found their tribe, built momentum through marketing brilliance and the business that started online had grown to print houses, production facilities and design teams. And they were still growing. But multiple companies and complex operational processes meant they had really outgrown the capabilities of Excel, which they had been relying on to run the business up to that point. They needed an ERP system and their operations lead had connected with us to work on this project.

The purpose of this project was to bring every process into a system, and at my first meeting the operations lead seemed clear on this purpose and appeared to have a mandate to get this moving. But as the project progressed, it became apparent that the business owner had somewhat abdicated the leading and purpose component of the project and was expecting to receive a 'working system' tied up with a pretty bow without needing to engage or do much.

This is not a recipe for success. This mismatch of expectations was one of the most difficult failures of customer engagement I have ever experienced. I learned a lot from this. Most critical of which is that if someone (especially the project sponsor) has unrealistic expectations about being delivered a working system without having to put in much effort themselves then it's better to wait and educate rather than getting into 'doing' right away.

So you have to make the choice. Of course, fundamentally, there should be more than one software solution that **can** work for you. Which one, and how you go about making it work will be up to you and your team.

A few things to keep in mind as you look for a software partner:

1. **There's no such thing as perfect software.** There's just software that you've worked on and with long enough that you've made it work for you. Like an off-the-rack outfit, figuring out the right accessories, occasion and seasonality for your 'outfit' is part of making it yours.

2. **The processes and business rules that you implement with the software are just as important as the way the software works.** There are gaps in every implementation, and the key is to understand the gaps and figure out what you can do to bridge the gaps or rework the process so that they're not there anymore.

3. **Software alone doesn't solve a problem**. People and processes need to work with the software and the implementation to set the project up for success.

4. **Balance the process with the functional ability of the software.** If the process is worthy, a competitive advantage or drives critical elements of your business, then it's worth keeping, and that should be clear from the start.

5. **Your teams will inherit the system and work with it once it's live.** Including them in early discussions and requirements assembling is a way to both improve the accuracy of your brief to any prospective vendor AND to build team momentum around the change or selection of a new system. Transparency and open communication are vital here.

6.   **The people who work in your business know more than any external experts ever will.** They are on the ground doing the doing of serving customers and delivering your product and service. Their knowledge and understanding of where you are right now, when engaged right, will smooth the path to future systems that work.

7.   **Do not undervalue the importance of decision-making agency.** How many people do you know who enjoy having choices forced upon them? Most people who are motivated enough to think about new systems and how to improve their business processes are not keen to be told how. Making decisions for people never makes them feel like they own it. Agency in the decision-making process gives the business team ownership over the choice. This is particularly valuable and useful at points in the implementation process where everyone wants to give up because something is not working.

8.   **Balance internal knowledge with external experience.** No one is an island, and we can all do with a different perspective to allow us to think about how we might tackle a problem or a situation in a new way. External experts can be a great way to get a new point of view or increase the capacity in your team, but external parties don't work in the business every day. Final decisions should *always* be with your team.

9.   **Be ready to be decisive.** Whether your whole team agrees on the right system for your business or not, someone needs to be prepared to cast the deciding vote and make the final decision.

The practice of understanding priorities, aligning internal people and getting everyone clear on what's most important is a stepping stone to project delivery work. It must start in the early stages of system and vendor partner selection.

What's the best system for us?

In my day-to-day practice, this question comes up frequently. Without really knowing who you are and what you're trying to do, it's impossible to answer well.

It all depends on a few things:

- what you mean by 'best'
- what is already working well in your business
- what you can afford or not afford to do and not do

Let's start with 'best'

A Google trends report from 2021 has some interesting comments on the word 'best' when used as a word to refine search results. The report highlights the decline of quantifiable terms like 'cheap' and the rise of the more subjective 'best'.[120] Search trends for 2023, highlight that people are becoming increasingly discerning, focusing on value beyond just price, including factors like brand trust and sustainability.[121] This reflects a continuation of the trend where consumers search for the 'best' options, not just the cheapest.

When people ask what is the best system, they're not necessarily asking what is the fastest or cheapest or easiest to implement. Best might refer to quality, value, performance, price or a combination of these and other measures. Because of that 'what is best' is more nuanced and personal

---

120   Rennie, A et al. 'Decoding Decisions: Making sense of the messy middle.' Think with Google. https://www.thinkwithgoogle.com/_qs/documents/9998/Decoding_Decisions_The_Messy_Middle_of_Purchase_Behavior.pdf.

121   Year in Search 2023. Google. https://about.google/stories/year-in-search/?utm_source=about_yis_hub&utm_medium=google_oo&utm_campaign=us; Thoma, S. (January 2023). 'From solar panels to spa days, see how 2022's top searches set the stage for 2023.' Think with Google. https://www.thinkwithgoogle.com/marketing-strategies/search/2022-insights/.

than a black and white measure like cheapest. The rise of what is 'best' in search terms points to our rise in tolerance for complexity and our desire for a greater understanding of our specific needs when receiving recommendations.

Increase in complexity

If you want to increase complexity, just add humans! I can't remember who said it, but this phrase has stuck with me, and I'm reminded of it nearly every day of my working life. In fact, researchers have found that humans will create more complexity in problem-solving tasks because our natural inclination is to add elements to solutions, rather than take any elements away.[122] It appears it's human nature.

Just recently, when working with a retailer, I had the finance lead confirm that there had been a re-forecast completed for the second half of the year. In the space of less than twenty-four hours the merchandise lead confirmed that there had **not** been a re-forecast for the second half of the year.

As it turned out, they were both correct.

How, you say?

It turns out they had very different understandings of what was meant by 're-forecast'. The finance leader was referring to some small changes to cost management and additional spend. The merchandise leader was referring to some seven figure changes that had been put forward and

---

122 Meyvis, T & Yoon, H. (7 April 2021). 'Adding is favoured over subtracting in problem solving.' *Nature*. https://www.nature.com/articles/d41586-021-00592-0.

decided against. This is a great example of why it's wise to ask the same question of multiple people to confirm your understanding.

System interactions are similar when it comes to complexity. The more systems you have the more integration points you have. The more integrations you have the more potential 'failure points' must not fail to make things work. The more systems you have the more vendors you must manage.

You can see where I'm going here, right?

Complexity increases when more data exchanges and partners are involved.

Deep or wide? What's right for you?

The temptation for business leaders who are in the stage of software selection is to see too many demonstrations and get too excited about all of them. What we often see in the selection phase is that people can get a bit mesmerised by all the shiny, new, exciting systems that appear to do things so much better than their current ones. They talk to multiple prospective vendor partners and are impressed. It can get confusing and hard to keep track of what the vendors are all offering and doing, and it's very easy, in the pressure of this situation, to skim over the surface instead of going deep.

Don't get me wrong, it's important to continue to educate yourself about what new innovations are taking place in your industry or what new tools are now on the market that you might take advantage of. But you need to balance that with getting the maximum possible value from the tools you already have.

It reminds me of a situation where I was pulled aside by the vendor partner in the first discovery meeting for what felt like some type of emergency summit. Contracts had been signed, and we were re-setting with the team prior to commencing the work on establishing new EDM software (used for automating email and building what digital marketers refer to as campaigns). Campaigns for this business were not just the pretty front end that winds up in your junk email. They also used this software to segment customers to know who had purchased recently (and, therefore, would not want to hear from them for a while) and who might be interested in their latest product launch.

The client had been using this tool for years, and they had become very adept at it. They had gone very deep into how to make it work for them and for their customers. They ran two big promotions each year, and this piece of software was a large contributor to the success of their half-year promotions. However, it was also part of the business that hadn't had a lot of technology investment for a while and the version they were using was quite old.

In our discovery session, we had all the business experts in the room, as well as the project manager, solution architect and business analyst from the vendor. At the end of the first meeting, the project manager from the vendor pulled me aside in a very urgent and confidential way. It turned out he was very concerned about the business' software selection.

He said to me, 'I don't know what to tell you, but they (the client) cannot continue to use this tool as a CRM (customer relationship management). It is not intended to be used that way.'

'What are you expecting me to do?' I asked,

'They need to invest in a CRM,' he said.

'Well, let's get this delivered first,' I responded, 'and we can then talk about a CRM.'

'They don't have a CRM,' he said. 'They're using this as though it is a CRM, and it's not designed for what they're using it for.'

He was right.

They had figured out a way of using it that meant that they really got what they needed out of it. Because they didn't have CRM, they added quite a few custom fields to give them greater insights for developing their campaigns. They sure were getting great value out of the software! But they had pushed it to the limits of what it was supposed to do and a little bit more.

As this story highlights, there's a balancing act here. You must walk a careful line. Trying to get a piece of software to do something that it's not designed to do is not wise. If you're fundamentally pushing against the grain of how the tool is designed, you're just making pain for you, your customers and the vendor.

This client and situation, however, was a bit more nuanced.

The thing that they were doing was **adjacent** to what this software was designed to do. So, they weren't pushing hard against the natural flow of the tool. They were just increasing the use of the tool to the point where they were really extracting a huge amount of value for themselves (given that they didn't have a CRM tool, they were making the best of what they did have). I think the vendor was so alarmed because they were concerned that they would somehow be implicated or held responsible for what the client was doing.

But the client was simply making the most of the existing system that they had. And it was a great solution that worked well for their unique business needs. I genuinely wish that I had more examples of this type of solution and decision-making than I do. It's easy to get excited about something new. (I'm as guilty of this as the next person, signing up for new exciting courses before I've finished the last one.) It's easy to forget that going deep into the tool that you already own can reap a lot of benefits.

The benefits of going deep

1. You already own it, so there are no barriers to experimentation except your own time and imagination. There are no business cases to sign off on or other parties to get involved. In most cases, you can conduct some discrete trials as well.

2. You have some skills in it. Learning how to do new things with an existing tool builds on the skills that you already have, rather than forcing you and your team to learn a new set from the ground up.

3. Not always, but occasionally, customers use a tool in such a way that it inspires the vendor or development team to build out a new feature or functional area that satisfies the need. This has the added benefit of saving you the additional work required to bring on a new piece of software.

4. There are fewer integration points and vendors to manage. In theory, getting more out of an existing vendor or system means that you're not taking data from one system and moving it to another. However, in practice this can sometimes be misleading. Where vendors increase their functionality through acquisition, it can mean that they have the same outside branding but different tech under the hood, so 'adding a module' from the same vendor might not mean a fully integrated solution.

The benefits of going wide

Of course, there are also benefits to going 'wide' or what is often referred to as getting 'best of breed'. This is where the customer chooses the best system for each function (ERP, commerce, customer and so on).

1. Get the best tool for the job, and no quibbles about it. Functional areas have what they need to get their job done, and no one has to compromise.

2. Spread the risk across multiple vendors and systems. If one is out, then hopefully there's enough goodwill in the world that they don't all go out (although pandemic days have made me think differently about the spread of risk).

3. Reduce the load on any one system. Each system can function independently and exchange information when it's needed, reducing reliance on one or two central systems.

4. With the right middleware, this approach can be very effective. However, the business rules and ongoing management of middleware must then be built into the ongoing management of the systems.

Choosing deep or wide

I'm a bit biased towards value, so I will always try to get as much as possible out of an existing system before adding plugins or new tools to the list. Going deep can give you amazing results. It's a little bit like somebody who snorkels at the surface seeing not much but murky water, versus the free diver who not only sees all the incredible sealife, but ends up with pearls as well.

What I will say about the balance of deep and wide approaches to systems is that in the early stages of business growth the deep strategy is probably the best one for you. If you're selecting your first ERP, try and get as much functionality out of it as you possibly can. Develop your processes around its strengths. If your business grows there will come a time when plugging the gaps will mean a business case for a system that is expert in something that your ERP doesn't do.

What's in the middle?

Every software system and solution is different. Some have out of the box connectors, some have APIs, some don't have much at all. This is where we start to get into the territory of middleware, which is a whole system in and of itself. If the organisation is large enough, then middleware might be something that you also need to consider as part of your systems selection process. Just remember that unless you are also outsourcing the management of the middleware, you'll need in-house experts to own that system as well. And unless you've invested in robust and reliable middleware the connecting pieces between said systems are always going to be the 'weakest link'.

As you work through the selection process you'll want to know if the system you're evaluating works with existing systems you intend to keep. Usually, the question decision makers ask the vendor is, 'Does it have an integration to [fill in your desired system here]?'

This is where things can get a bit fuzzy...

The integration rainbow

Integration is one of those words, a little bit like spaghetti. It has as many interpretations as spaghetti does for the people who make it. When I'm describing this to clients who are not familiar with what integration can mean in its many different guises, I say, 'It's a rainbow.'

Not literally a rainbow. I do not mean, 'a display of the colours of the spectrum produced by the dispersion of light'[123] nor 'a wide range of related and typically colourful things.'[124] Instead I use the word to help us see how integration has some of the ephemeral qualities of the rainbow, in that it can be difficult to see and capture. If you'll indulge me a little here…

- **Red** on the rainbow is an integration that doesn't really exist. Perhaps it has been imagined in the mind of the vendor, and there are some rough diagrams about how it might work in someone's notebook. However, it's not useful to you until it's working and passing data.

- An **orange** integration is one that passes key data from one system to another. It sounds quite useful. But if it doesn't update data after the first pass, then you will need to build some processes around making sure the systems stay in sync with each other.

- A **yellow** integration could be one that passes information from one system to another and then updates the originating system if something changes.

- If we take this a step further, a **green** version might also include in-built alerts to let the right user know about a change in data between systems.

- A **blue** one might include business logic that you can edit and update as business logic changes.

123 Oxford English Dictionary. (n.d.). Rainbow. In *Oxford English Dictionary*. https://www.oed.com/dictionary/rainbow_n?tl=true.

124 Oxford Languages. (n.d.). Colourful. In *Google* via Oxford Languages. https://www.google.com/search?sca_esv=6c359354a686a14b&q=colourful&si=AKbGX_rLPMd HnrrwkrRo4VZlSHiJz4aqExsag1GTrmmQJ12TAUNnvdzhuy44ncmK1zKTPy27qA0 wf8rhUvFJy4WoAhpPogfKWPjY4Qi-JE4DYntlMM0cJ38%3D&expnd=1.

- An **indigo** one could also include the capability to automatically retry after a certain period of time.
- Maybe a **violet** integration includes some monitoring capability for performance or speed.

Clearly, this is not a comprehensive or complete list of all the things that integrations do. It's intended as an example of the range of interpretations that are there for how software is integrated. When customers ask vendors, 'Is this system integrated with another system that I already have?' and vendors answer, 'yes', they could be answering yes to any one of the colours in that rainbow and fully believe it's the honest answer despite it perhaps not really fulfilling the type of integration that you need for your business.

Working well (and working with others)

Most systems that have been around for a while and have a solid customer base work well discretely. By discretely, I mean within themselves. That doesn't mean that they necessarily connect to other systems or play nicely with anything that you are already using.

In terms of what type of integrations you need for different systems, it will depend on the number of transactions that are being passed between the systems and the type of business logic that's required to keep each system maintaining its own core logic in a solid working fashion. So, as you can imagine, and maybe have experienced for yourself, integration can be the hidden hell of a project. In fact, integration can be the thing that brings implementations undone in terms of estimate, effort and expectation management.

In a recent project that we worked on, the client had chosen three key systems (and vendors): one for POS retail, one for ERP and one for e-commerce. The integration responsibility sat with the ERP vendor.

When the vendor sold the solution to the client, they assured the client that integrations already existed between the ERP and one of the other systems. As it turned out, the integration was probably more on the red-orange end of the rainbow, while the client had expectations on the blue-indigo end of the colour spectrum.

This misunderstanding resulted in significant blowouts in time and cost for this project. Other aspects of the project were delayed because there were dependencies on the integration. It needed to be working to be able to pass data between systems and commence testing. There were a lot of other factors that influenced this situation, but it's worth calling out how easy it is for integration mishaps to derail an entire project, particularly one where you've got multiple vendors involved. Once momentum is lost, it's very hard to rebuild it.

Understand what type of integration the vendor is offering

Sometimes the vendor will supply an existing one-to-one integration where you can drag and drop fields and match them between the systems. This can be very helpful for you to identify where you want to pass data or how you want to match the logic.

Other systems have more workflow tools inside them where you can create workflows with business logic inside them yourself. You might need some more technically-minded humans on your team to help with this type. Other integrations work on layers of logic, building system connections and then business logic at a higher level. The advantage of this is that you don't have to do too much work on the system connection layer to reuse the logic multiple times. The usefulness of this, of course, depends on what systems you're connecting to and how mature your business is.

Be prepared for implementing integrations

Integrations can get a bit lost in the sales stage of the selection of new systems, so I'm calling it out here as something to keep in mind. Be aware that this can take as much effort as system implementation and that the earlier you think about it and put some plans around it, the better prepared you will be.

A couple of small tips here. If you're not sure what the integration looks like, then ask for a technical specification from the vendor. The more complete and comprehensive this document is, the more evolved the integration is. It should be what is already built. If they can't supply a technical specification, then it means it's definitely more towards the red end of the spectrum than the blue end of the spectrum.

> **If you're not sure what the integration looks like, then ask for a technical specification from the vendor.**

No matter which integration approach you choose, there is one clear rule. You (or someone on your team) must understand how it works.

Tips on selecting your software system

Selecting your software system can be its own mini project effort (depending on the size of the business). When you're looking for a new tool, it requires an amount of energy to establish what you need, understand if the new software will 'play nicely' with the things that already work in your business, develop a business case and get it signed off. And once you're at the end of this process, you haven't even gotten it out of the packet yet. You've only been given permission to implement.

You can make this process a bit smoother by considering the following:

Explore & evaluate

As consumers, we bounce around in what Google researchers have called the 'messy middle'.[125] 'Consumers explore their options and expand their knowledge and consideration sets, then – either sequentially or simultaneously – they evaluate the options and narrow down their choices.' [126]

Reading this, I was reminded of my recent search for an oven. To do it I explored the brands that were out there, where they were manufactured, their quality reputation, their cooking capabilities and their features. This was the 'explore' phase. Once I had this information, I was able to compare and evaluate. Some sites have made the comparison process easy by putting products side by side in an easy evaluation tool. Others haven't. To make my choice, I went back and forth between ratings and comparison sites and asking for advice from family and friends until I felt I had the right data to make a decision.

The same process holds true for finding business systems that are 'best' for you. The explore and evaluate model follows a 'design thinking' expansion of ideas and imagination and then the honing in on options to compare and evaluate. This process should be repeated multiple times through the system selection, implementation and refinement of systems use, as you gather more data and information through the process.

It's worth keeping in mind as you explore and evaluate that this is not 'the end'. There will (possibly) be another round of this – maybe not immediately. But the path to continuous improvement, which is the path

---

125 Rennie. Decoding Decisions.
126 Rennie. Decoding Decisions.

that we're always on, is a path of re-examining your assumptions and refining your choices.

Researching your own business

In preparation for a new system the business team will undertake work to confirm understanding of their current processes, document where the pain points are and have a reference point to explain existing processes to external experts and vendor partners.

The work of aligning needs and how those needs work together is excellent preparation for the work needed in project delivery. It's typical that functional areas in a business have their own perspective and may not have considered the whole flow end to end.

Reviewing each functional area's requirements as one cohesive whole and understanding what you need for your business overall can be a big job. But it's also one that hopefully brings the team closer to a shared understanding about what's going on right now, and the biggest ticket items to improve. It also helps internal teams align and get clarity on all the elements that need to work in harmony.

Making the choice [8 steps]

Having the right people around you and on your team can make everything a lot easier and work a lot more smoothly. And if you have the wrong people around you, it can make for a grating, protracted and difficult time. The point here is that this is not a one day engagement for you.

So when you select software vendors it's with the understanding that this will be a working relationship that will stand for the length of time that the system is in place. Depending on the system that could be between five and seven years. And when it comes to ERP systems it will very likely be a lot longer than that, which means you want to make sure you get the right partner on board.

So, here's the eight-step process that we recommend when we're helping clients find the right partner.

1. **What you have now.** The first step is to examine your own processes. When you examine your own processes, you need to ensure that you're not holding on too tight. Give the space to question and examine all the processes that you have and see what you can stop doing. That's always my favourite way to save some time. Ask yourself, 'what do I need to not do anymore and really optimise? What are the friction points that, if solved, will make the biggest difference?'

2. **Your future needs.** The second step is usually to consider the future needs or plans for the business. If you have a three to five year plan or a big goal on the horizon, think about your systems with that future goal in mind. Do you have the systems in place that will support that goal?

3. **What is staying?** Which systems are already working well? Maybe you've got an e-commerce site that is already kicking goals and you know that you want to keep that platform, or you've only just replaced it. Whatever else you implement will need to work with the system that's bedded down and working. This is also a magnificent way to hone down your list of suppliers. If the partner doesn't work with the system that you've already said is a keeper, then put it further down the list. Of course, if you really do love the new software, there's always the option to build an integration piece. Just make sure you've allowed enough time and effort for that.

4. **Your non-negotiables.** We then have a bunch of key partner questions. Basically, we're looking for the items you know about that are 'not negotiable'. Do you want to host on premises or in the cloud? Do you need local support? Do you want a system that has multiple levels of hierarchy or product structure? A few key decision points can also help refine the list.

5. **Book demonstrations.** If it's at all possible, try to give vendors some of your own data so that they can do a demo with your data. This has the added benefit of letting the vendor see some of your data and get familiar with the structure and naming conventions in your business.

6. **Set up your scorecard.** Set up an evaluation matrix (scorecard) for the systems and partners, and make sure that you involve a few people from the business in the evaluation process. Complete the evaluation form for each vendor as close as possible to the demonstration.

7. **Decide.** Before you decide, make it clear to your team how the decision will be made. I often see a group of key users and stakeholders involved in the decision making but with one person having the ultimate approval. Don't give people the impression that the decision is theirs if it's not.

8. **Respond.** This last step is critically important. Go back to everyone on the vendor list and let them know what software you've chosen. Don't leave them hanging with no response. It's just good manners. Apart from being good manners, it's entirely possible that things may go wrong with the software that you've chosen. I've seen situations where a vendor has been appointed and then they get acquired or the business takes on a new direction, and the selection decision is revisited. You don't want to burn any bridges if you can help it. And it's

so much easier to re-open a conversation if you completed the selection process by letting those who were not successful know that they were not.

Vendor cautions

Chatting to someone I had just met at a business breakfast, we were 'finding common ground' as you do when you first meet. She shared that her organisation is undergoing a significant software change project. They have appointed a vendor and are in the process of replacing 55 legacy systems (that's a lot). They've selected a tier one software provider and they've got experts coming out of every orifice. But still, there was this disappointment about how the process was going. The gap between what they've been sold and what they must do to get it anywhere NEAR working the way they believed it would was not clear to her from the outset and the effort ahead was starting to dawn on her.

Unfortunately, I've seen this 'software disappointment' before. It happens all the time in software projects, and you can see how.

Disappointment comes from unmet expectations – the more significant the expectations, the more significant the disappointment. When it comes to engaging with vendors to deliver significant business systems, the expectations are huge, and not every retail business is great at articulating these expectations.

> Disappointment comes from unmet expectations – the more significant the expectations, the more significant the disappointment.

In the early stages of a software project, expectations are often referred to as requirements. When selecting your software and appointing the vendor you need to take an active role. They will not be able to complete an implementation without you and your team. Some observations and cautions here to set you up for a productive working relationship.

Vendor promises to be wary of

We know it works in business X, and it'll do the same thing for you.

This kind of promise relies on a vendor assumption (or presumption) that your business is the same as this other business and builds your expectation that things will work in the same way because of it. This is rarely true. Even in the same industry, each business can present differently.

It's very hard to pick up a process that serves one organisation and parachute it into a different one. It rarely works because it's not connected to the same combination of systems, processes and culture. The process, the nature of the business and the intentions are rarely an easy swap in and out.

Even if this promise feels like it should work, test the assumption. Find out what is the same or different about this situation and the vendor's previous experience with the other client? What similarities does our business have to business X? How is their culture the same or different? Dig in to find out more.

We can meet your timelines. (Here is our perfectly presented vendor activity.)

Explainer decks, where vendors are presenting to a potential client, present a timeline that explains what they (the vendor) are going to do and how long it should take. These pretty presentations rarely articulate what the client business team will need to do and what those people need to bring to the situation. It's an example of the 'perfect' project where everyone is ready and knows exactly what they need to do (and has the time to do it).

A vendor cannot complete a project without some cooperation and input from the whole business from the leadership level to people who will be using the software. If the business activities are not considered in the timeline, it's a warning sign that the timeline is incomplete. Don't let yourself get attached to these high level ideal timelines.

To test the perfect timeline that is presented, ask which activities can be completed without your business input. If you cannot provide information, data or business knowledge, at a certain time what impact will this have on the timeline? Try asking what the vendor will need from you at each stage of the project.

We can give you a better deal! (A vendor suddenly drops their price for no apparent reason.)

When choosing a system most business owners look to the market to understand what's on offer and what best fits their business. Vendors present and estimate to their best knowledge what's feasible.

When one vendor's price drops without any explanation as to why or how it usually means that you (the client) are compromising on something (and it often means that they've seen what their competitors are offering and drop their prices to match). What's often not clear is what the compromise is. Selecting on price alone is never a good strategy but everyone has to work with constraints, budget being a big one.

When a vendor suddenly drops their prices, ask what the vendor is not doing or not including or changing to make this new price work. Has a critical must-do function been dropped or the more desirable thing that you can't (or don't want to) cope without?

Even when we see business teams make the most incredibly detailed effort to brief a vendor properly, gaps can still happen. Maybe the vendor has not sufficiently appreciated how important something is to the business teams and (wrongly) expected to be able to replace it with something simpler that doesn't do the whole job.

The best way to close this gap is to ask questions. And keep asking questions until you've run out. Knowing the right questions to ask can be tricky if you haven't worked with vendors before.

You're ready to choose your software

As you close out phase 1, it's clear that choosing the right software is not just a technical decision – it's also a strategic and cultural one. The selection process is where your vision begins to take shape, but it's also where potential pitfalls can first appear. Finding the right system fit for you is as much about understanding your own business needs as it is about evaluating what the market and the various partners have to offer.

The key takeaway from this phase is that the decision must be yours, rooted in a deep understanding of both current operations and future goals (even those in the long distance future). This will set the stage for a successful implementation and, ultimately, the realisation of the system's full potential. Now you're ready to move into the next phase, where the real work begins – bringing that system to life within your organisation.

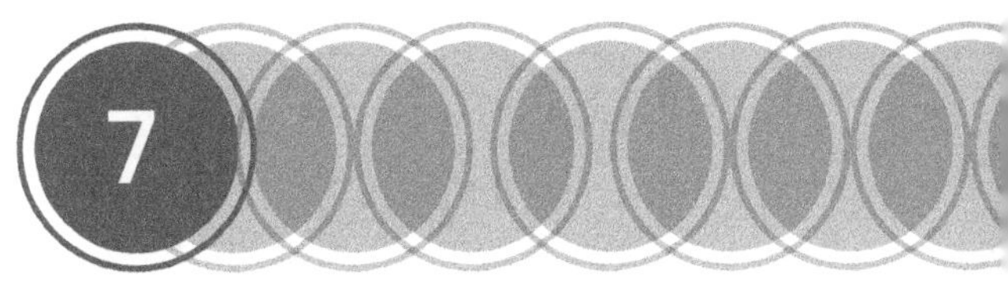

Action (Part 2)

Phase 1 – software implementation – was a big part of taking action in a change project. But we're not done yet. Next comes phase 2, software implementation and phase 3, learning how to really use the software.

PHASE 2: Software implementation – making a plan of action

As we get into initiating a project, meaning that it has a clear business case and a green light on funding, we then move into the getting things done stage. This part might be called the Nike part of the project – the 'just do it' phase.

But the reality is that before we can 'just do it' we need a shared plan.

The plan of action cycle

A lot of the stage setting, the higher purpose strategic and purpose work around scope and roles and so on, has been done or is in progress to bring everyone and everything project related into alignment. But as we are building alignment around a project, we'll also be developing a plan of action (or a POA).

As we've seen in previous chapters, alignment and planning is a big piece of work at the beginning of any project implementation. But even when that is finished, we have to continue to plan and replan in smaller ways to ensure we're on track throughout the life of the project.

Your implementation plan is not a one-and-done kind of thing. A POA for me follows a series of steps that repeats over and over as needed to form a circle or cycle.

So what does this look like? The first step is to plan. The second is when we move on to doing. And while the doing is in full swing, we implement the third step, monitoring. Monitoring ensures that we're sticking to our plan and completing the pieces that need doing along the way. But it also ensures that we're replanning as needed. And once we 'replan' we move back into doing, then monitoring, then replanning once more. And so it continues to go until the project implementation is complete.

The Plan of Action Cycle

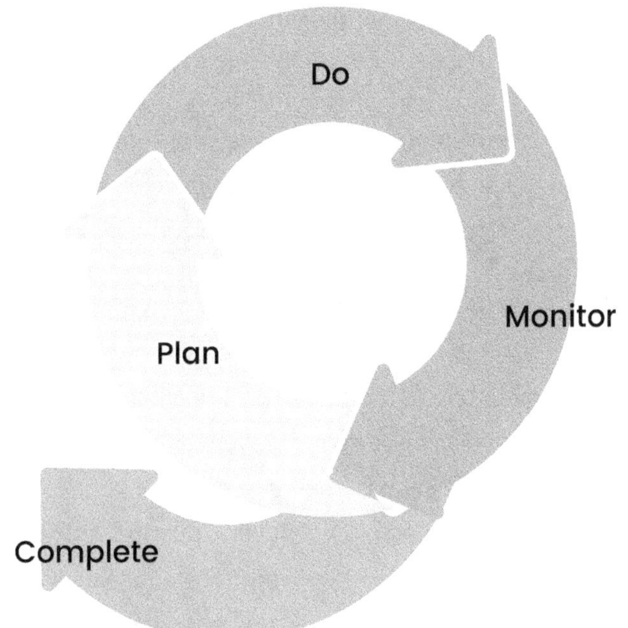

Step 1, your POA

To build a plan of action, we need strategy, transparency and clear communication (which we've talked about in detail in previous chapters). When it comes to building our action plan the strategy revolves around understanding how this effort fits into our big picture goals. This informs both what we do and what we don't do, and informs the scope and requirements of the project.

Transparency within the action plan requires us to be able to freely share information across the core project team and build ways of working that engender trust while we're doing the doing and monitoring the doing as well.

Clarity in communicating requirements is one of the most critical foundation elements of your project, and therefore of your action plan. As you move further along your project, you'll add people to the project and your communication lines need to increase as well.

Beyond these three elements, there's a wealth of knowledge out there in the world around methodologies and approaches to planning the action part of projects. In fact, it's the piece of project work that people are most familiar with.

Despite all the available information, too often an action plan is built around what amounts to a fantasy. Just like fantasy football, in your fantasy action plan, all your preferred players are injury free and can be on your team. The timeline has been thought up in a magical fairyland where there are no clashes of schedules, everyone is available when needed, your day-to-day business work moves ahead easily and no other pressing emergencies arise. In this land, there are no conflicts, shortages of equipment or shipping problems. No one gets sick, no one's cat dies, no one moves house, no one has a car accident and no one gets pregnant. There are no children or parents that require extra care, attention or rescue from unexpected mishaps. And there is no way this is ever going to happen outside of our magical fairyland.

It sounds ridiculous, but so often it feels like this is how project timelines are estimated, and it won't surprise you to hear that it's usually not by the people who will be doing the actual work. But building an action plan around a fantasy timeline just leaves lots of room for disappointment.

Most of us are not good at estimating, and it's not our fault.

Consider the construction of the Sydney Opera House. The original estimates were made in 1957, and the planners estimated it would cost

US$7 million to build and be completed in four years. But the reality was it cost over US$102 million to build and took 14 years to complete.[127]

This is called the 'planning fallacy'.[128] It's a phenomenon where we consistently underestimate the time (and/or cost) a future task will take to complete due to our inherent optimism bias (the difference between the person's expectation and the outcome).[129] It's human nature – how our brains are wired. Everyone thinks that they can do things faster than they can, for example, write a book (I'm looking in the mirror here!) and certainly make an action plan.

So, our job is to try and combat the optimism bias when we're planning. This means working hard to test and push back against fantasyland assumptions.

Here are four things that can help:

1. Consult widely

Consult widely (and wisely). One of the things that we like to do when we're building a detailed plan is to consult widely with the people who will actually be doing the work. If they aren't available or haven't been recruited yet, then we look for someone who has done this type of work (or similar) before to build an estimate.

---

127 'Our story: Construction begins.' Sydney Opera House. https://www.sydneyoperahouse.com/our-story/construction-begins.

128 Buehler, R, Griffin, D & Peetz, J. (2010). 'Chapter One – The Planning Fallacy: Cognitive, Motivational and Social Origins.' *Advances in Experimental Social Psychology.* https://www.sciencedirect.com/science/article/abs/pii/S0065260110430014.

129 Sharot, T. (6 December 2011). 'The optimism bias.' *Current Biology.* https://www.sciencedirect.com/science/article/pii/S0960982211011912#:~:text=The%20optimism%20bias%20is%20defined,expected%2C%20the%20bias%20is%20pessimistic.

When the person who is doing it is on the team, reviewing the estimated time allowed with them is part of their onboarding. This serves two purposes. First, it guards against the 'you never asked me' indignation that people can rightly feel when a deadline is imposed. Second, it starts to build a level of personal commitment within the team.

2. Create some contingency

As well as consulting, we usually try to allow for some contingency. I often think of this as being a bit like the Canadian Children's Hospital. This hospital implemented a dedicated operating room (OR) for emergency cases, thereby improving the quality of care for both elective and emergency surgery. While no one knew what emergencies there would be, they knew there would be emergencies – it's a hospital after all. So, giving dedicated space for these allowed for better budget planning and staffing for the OR. A study on how this created better outcomes for the hospital demonstrated that the cancellation of elective cases due to emergency cases decreased significantly.[130]

Similarly, in projects, if we allow contingency for the imperfections of life and availability, we reduce the need to re-allocate people to emergencies, which will certainly arise. These contingencies will reduce the friction and interruptions to the flow of work. Areas that are less known or more complex are the obvious places to build in contingency time or budget since they're more likely to see those emergencies arise.

3. Find capacity

Part of building your action plan is making sure you have the right capacity within your team. You'll need to consider the specialist roles in

---

130 Heng, M & Wright, J. (June 21013). 'Dedicated operating room for emergency surgery improves access and efficiency.' *Canadian Journal of Surgery.* https://www. ncbi.nlm.nih.gov/pmc/articles/PMC3672429/.

your business. Part of building a plan is figuring out how team members will create capacity for themselves, what they're doing inside their own teams to build capacity to spend time on a project and how to free up capacity inside the business to allow for the project work to take place. You will likely need to find additional support or reduce other workloads to make space for your project work as part of building capacity in your team.

A plan is not a timeline

One more note on planning. A plan is not a timeline. But your plan must *have* a timeline.

A timeline is an essential document for a project. It shows the series of tasks and milestones that will help guide your progress. Your timeline helps everyone stay aligned and understand how and where to schedule interdependent activities.

The timeline supports your ability to see your progress, but it doesn't show a complete picture. A project plan does. It explains the how. I often think of the plan as the rules of engagement or the guardrails that we're putting around the way that the team will work. A plan should include the purpose of the project as well as the expected measures of success. It should state who will do the work and how the work will get done. It should set out constraints, risks, how you will communicate and how you can escalate any stuck items for resolution. A timeline is part of this, but it's not everything we need.

The outcome of the early planning phase of a project is that no matter what methods we use and partners we're working with, the plan should roll up to a shared set of outcomes by certain times that are agreed upon. And the whole team must be clear on what the outcomes are for each milestone and how they will reach them.

Step 2, doing

So now we're finally ready to move into the 'doing' and monitoring phases of our implementation. And when it comes to the 'doing' of the implementation of the change project, a big part is understanding how to manage your resources during the life of your project.

Managing your resources

The best way to manage project resources is by developing repeatability, rhythm and risk management within your project. But when it comes to 'resources' what are we referring to? Resources are anything your project needs to be completed successfully. Often in projects this includes tech, data, information, materials, partners, financial capital and even people.

> The best way to manage project resources is by developing repeatability, rhythm and risk management within your project.

One of my pet peeves about project language, however, is that we often refer to people as resources rather than people. It feels like we are dehumanising one of the most valuable parts of a project when we talk about people as resources. Chris Voss, an ex-FBI negotiator who teaches negotiation, shares in an interview with Andrew Huberman of Huberman Lab that if you ever find yourself in a hostage situation, finding a way to humanise yourself by sharing your name with the hostage taker will increase your chances of survival.[131] Huberman adds to this by describing how scientists are strongly advised to give primates that

---

131 Huberman, A. (2 October 2023). Chris Voss: How to Succeed at Hard Conversations [Video]. Huberman Lab. https://www.youtube.com/watch?v=q8CHXefn7B4.

they are experimenting on numbers, not names.[132] In *Monsters Inc.*, Mike groans when he realises that Sully has given the terrifying human child a name.[133]

When we dehumanise our people by referring to them as 'capital' we lower their ability to have real impact and we take away value around their individual intelligence and insights (that go far beyond their role or responsibility). This is not the recipe for success. Instead, when we think about resourcing, we should be looking beyond the human parts of the project work and considering other aspects of the project that we need to manage too.

Resourcing also means access to the tools and systems required to do the work. Things like hardware, environments, licences and access to information. A lot of that stuff actually builds out the structure of our project and the ways that we're working. And when they're repeatable we're better able to manage them.

Repeatability & rhythm

A repeatable rhythm means that things happen at a certain time and in a certain way. It allows people to build habits and block time for the work they're going to need to do and sets the tone for the entire project. So, a repeatable rhythm might be daily or weekly stand ups or meetings where each project contributor provides updates against the plan.

Of course, that rhythm can be adjusted as the project evolves. Sometimes, instead of getting together to review the work, it's better to make time to do the work. Adapt the flow and adjust as needed throughout the project.

---

132 Huberman. Chris Voss.
133 Doctor, P. (Director). (2001). *Monsters, Inc.* [Film]. Pixar Animation Studios for Walt Disney Pictures.

Timely action

When we have to stop, switch tasks or pick up a new thread of conversation, we lose momentum in the work that we are focused on.[134] There is substantial evidence that shows that the act of stopping, switching tasks and trying to resume previous work imposes significant cognitive and time costs. Project sponsors and project managers have a responsibility to take timely action on any risks or missing elements that would impact the momentum of the project.

It can cost us.

I have recent experience with project sponsors not appreciating the importance of ensuring that their team can focus on their project work. Whilst it was obvious to me as an external partner with the business, that there were team members who were not the right mix of skills and attitude for their project, they disagreed. They resisted removing a team member from the project because it felt like it was politically appropriate to include them. As a long serving member of the business leadership team, this person had a lot of cultural capital to offer to the project. As it turned out, they were not that interested in lending this cultural influence on the forward momentum of the project, and instead put efforts into disruption.

This is an example of where a lack of timely action by the project sponsor cost the project further down the path, distracting and disrupting the momentum that had been built with other team members.

---

134 (2006). 'Multitasking: Switching costs.' American Psychological Association. https://www.apa.org/topics/research/multitasking.

Step 3, monitoring

Developing practices that work will be unique to your project. Some of the monitoring processes we usually build into our implementation are: weekly 'in progress' checkpoints, change control conversations, risk management reviews and reporting and executive, sponsorship or board level progress tracking. This helps us find out what we've completed this period and what's planned for the next. The important thing is to get a routine and rhythm going. If it's not working, adjust.

When it comes to continuous monitoring and ongoing improvements we have some small internal rituals that we try to live by and help our clients with. For example, we try to have the project work focus on specific days and get into a groove of working on those days each week. Since I work with a lot of retailers these tend to be 'not Monday', i.e. following the weekend trade. This allows a team to get into a working rhythm, and as part of this we usually complete our reporting on Fridays. It's a good way to review the week and take action on anything that has slipped off track.

Part of the monitoring process is to always have an eye for risk and keeping lines of communication open so that you can build out mitigation strategies. When it comes to ensuring that you've got a good handle on the risks of your project, starting with lessons learned from previous projects or connecting with other project managers inside an organisation and understanding what they're working on will help. I always ask for input from all project participants, including vendors when it comes to compiling risks. Often the vendor sees risk in quite a different way to the client.

When it comes to building out a risk management register you need to ensure that it's a standing agenda item to review it. It's also helpful to add to the weekly project meeting or stand up if there are any new risks to highlight.

One of the trickier risks to manage is, of course, key people's availability. So, we always ask for annual leave plans to be included in the project schedule. Typically managing and monitoring would include planning ahead at the individual level for some team members. Being close to their workload and what they have capacity for is an important part of building strong collaborative muscles.

If there are key team members who might be across multiple projects, ensuring that they've got visibility of their upcoming tasks and that they've created time to do the work is an important part of monitoring the project progress.

PHASE 3: Learning how to (really) use the software (Why 'live' doesn't mean 'done'!)

We delivered a **ship from store project** for a retailer during the pandemic. The unique situation meant there were urgent pressures to get the new systems up and running as quickly as possible. We worked with them to get the technology piece tested, stood up and working in two weeks.

It was a tough ask, but we got there.

After a push like that, getting something live and working in such a short space of time, it's easy to relax and think you're done. But honestly, the hard bit was just beginning – the reality of implementation is never as smooth as the theory.

The retailer soon found this out. The next four to six weeks were spent refining the process and working with the team who were learning to use the software. The day to day was about how things were communicated, the order and flow of the day and how to prioritise the influx of new work. We needed to clarify the metrics, make sure people were doing things correctly and following the designed and tested process.

That part of the project was a lot messier and involved more people, training, re-training, re-framing and re-working. It was an iterative process but one, in this situation, that was appropriate. The pressing need for the ship from store option in the midst of COVID lockdowns was a matter of continuing to make sales or not.

It's this piece around making operational bits work and align that is so often **undercooked** in project delivery.

Being prepared for post-live

Many businesses have found after they 'go live' they need the support of the project team almost *more* than they did when preparing for taking the project live. The work of the project continues in the form of becoming competent in the new systems and software, and, unfortunately, in almost all cases it's akin to climbing the next summit in a mountain range.

Here are some of the things we find that projects often need in the period immediately[135] post-live:

---

135 Usually vendors will have what they call a 'hypercare' period that starts immediately after go live when they are on alert for anything that has not worked out.

- Daily communication with the project team to review what is working and what is not. Over time this will likely taper off to once a week.

- Quick resolution of issues that crop up. Often this is resolved with process clarity and training, but it's useful to keep the vendor/s on standby to resolve problems as they come up (after all, they're part of the team too).

- Continuous reporting of progress against your original targets. Then you'll be able to see things improve (or not) each day or week and have clarity on whether or not you're meeting your targets and goals.

Sometimes issues can lie dormant for a few weeks. It's after the dust settles that we see the cracks of misunderstanding, things that didn't really work in the real world and just plain old mistakes. Keeping the project team knowledge at hand and having project experience around to help troubleshoot at this point makes the leap from project phase to operational much smoother.

Whenever you're embarking on something new, you're asking more of your people; creating the right support for them in the transition to operations is a critical part of ensuring your project success.

Hand off to operational teams

When therapists work with patients making changes to their lives and habits they have a cycle of change that they describe as a little bit like the 'stages of grief'. The change process has multiple phases, and they're not linear. In therapy the stage that often follows action is referred to as maintenance, this stage has an alternate option of relapse.

Research conducted by McKinsey indicates that this maintenance is hard to maintain. After three years often major transformation projects have still not stuck, and the use of the system(s) are not well embedded into operational working processes.

In our process, the best possible bridge to maintenance starts at the start of the project. We work to create cross functional teams that build candid communication, transparent and collaborative work methods and some agency over the change process. So, if we've included people early in the process and created space for a collaborative design process for future ways of working, what else do we need to do?

Developing networks that can train and support team members immediately post live really helps. Ensuring that team members have the time dedicated to come to training, can do basic functions on the system on day one and can utilise the forum to ask questions and troubleshoot any oddities also assist the transition to a new working process. Building out training guides for day one as well as cheat sheets as reminders helps (as daggy and old school as this sounds it's still useful). Training guides don't need to be documents, they can be videos, tooltips or even Q and A format. Where possible embedding the tips to the system where users will need them is a good way to make them accessible and easy to find when help is needed.

We need to ensure that the resistance part of our adoption to change is at a manageable level. So, ensuring that people get through any issues or problems that they experience in that post go live period quickly and with as little pain as possible builds confidence in the process and the new system. Creating daily or weekly check-ins to track any problems and the progress of resolution is important. Continuing the theme of communicating well, tracking any issues that we've found, how quickly they're being resolved, and then keeping everyone informed, gives people comfort that they've got the support that they need to build up to confidence in the new system.

In the immediate post live period we try to keep operational teams and project teams working side by side so that the operational team can take care of any project documents that need to be updated for 'real world' improvement.

System mastery

When my Dad implemented 'operation cooperation', the project had a firm set of parameters, processes and goals. But we were children. So a lot of these fell over in the doing. We just weren't very good at motivating ourselves, keeping ourselves accountable or just doing the tasks themselves. Using new software and tech to its best is often the same. Like operation cooperation, many fledgling systems will fall over before being able to really get full value from the new software.

So when it comes to post-live you're done. But you're not *done, done*. Now is the time to reflect, review and refine your systems set up, processes, integrations or automations. A 'mature' system is the goal. So project leaders must understand that not only will they need to implement the software, but they will also need to ensure the organisation can drive it well to really extract the value from it.

Complexity and maturity of systems

But what is a mature system? Just because something is complex doesn't mean it's mature. Mature, to us, is a marker for the depth of use businesses are getting from their systems. Are the systems being widely used? Is the data accurately maintained and relied on? Does everyone across the business buy into the same data? Or are there differences of opinion about whose numbers are 'right'? Mature uses of systems have extracted every bit of value that they can from their investment, just like our client who was using the EDM as a surrogate CRM.

Complexity is sometimes born of the desire to cater for every scenario in a process or from different people not consulting with one another end to end. It sounds counterintuitive but making a system simple is often a lot of really hard work at thinking through how people will interact with and use systems.

You can see how the simple system is the more mature, and the best for the organisation as a whole. Similarly, we want to see simpler, more robust systems in place to support your change project post live. But doing so is almost like taking on a secondary project – one that supports the real value of the first. It's not an easy summit to climb, but it's one that must be conquered.

Long-term thinking about ongoing improvements

James Clear says it well in his best selling book, *Atomic Habits* – it's not just about getting the project live, it's also about the ongoing improvement.

> 'True long-term thinking is goal less thinking. It's not about any single accomplishment. It is about the cycle of endless refinement and continuous improvement. Ultimately, it is your commitment to the process that will determine your progress.'[136]

The true test of your project's success lies not in going live, but in the days, weeks and months that follow. This is when the system is integrated

---

136 Clear, J. (2018). *Atomic Habits: Tiny Changes, Remarkable Results.* Century – Trade.

into daily operations, team members have adapted to new processes and the intended benefits of the software have begun to materialise.

Success is not merely about having the system in place. It's also about ensuring that it functions smoothly, enhances productivity, and truly aligns with your business objectives. By embracing this ongoing process, you not only secure the value of your initial project but also set the stage for long-term growth and efficiency, turning your software investment into a powerful tool for continuous improvement.

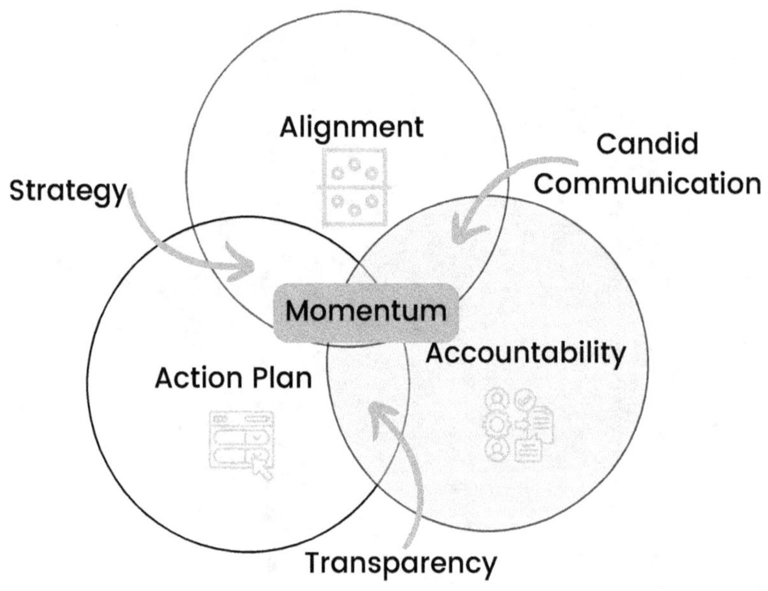

Alignment
Candid
Communication
Strategy
Momentum
Accountability
Action Plan
Transparency

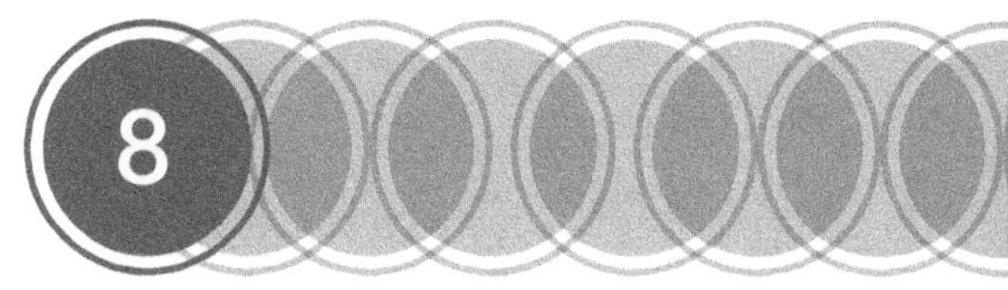

8

Accountability & Communication

Accountability, the commitment to honouring deadlines and responsibilities, is a cornerstone of effective project delivery. But it's also one of the trickiest aspects to master as it requires a delicate balance between personal discipline and the ability to navigate the complexities of team dynamics. Getting it right is about ensuring that it's a collective effort that builds trust and fosters a culture of reliability and high performance.

We can think of communication as the lifeblood that sustains accountability. As Brené Brown has so cleverly articulated, clear, compassionate and consistent communication is kind because it ensures that expectations are understood and issues are addressed promptly. Importantly, it also creates a pathway for everyone to remain aligned with the project's goals and to aspire to high standards.[137]

Accountability and communication matter because when they're done well in an organisation, outcomes can be fantastic. My son has

137   Brown, B. (15 October 2018). 'Clear is Kind. Unclear is Unkind.' Brené Brown. https://brenebrown.com/articles/2018/10/15/clear-is-kind-unclear-is-unkind/.

recently started his first job at a place where they've done this so well. The company makes and distributes gases, which has large public safety and risk attached. This team is dealing with things that have real, significant consequences in the physical world. So his onboarding had a lot of focus on safety and reducing waste, both admirable areas of attention in the supply chain area where he's working.

What's interesting about this onboarding process is that the chain of responsibility has been made explicitly clear to him. His part in the chain and the responsibility for public safety were impressed upon him from his first day working with the team. And the organisation's process made him, a new recruit, feel immediately personally responsible for getting things right, for checking what happens and for doing their best to balance both safety and optimisation of resources. The organisation has demonstrated that unique and beautiful marriage of accountability – both personal and organisational – with clear communication to convey their high standards and expectations.

Just like at my son's place of work, accountability and communication work hand in hand to create a project environment that is primed for success. So it's important to understand how to create the mindset and practical strategies to cultivate these practices within your teams.

Accountability

Project work, by its very definition, requires a team of people to get something big done. That means that somehow, we all need to honour a level of personal accountability within an accountable team environment. This matters because project teams that have high levels of accountability are more productive and generate work at a better quality.

So what is accountability? Webster's Dictionary defines accountability as 'an obligation or willingness to accept responsibility for one's actions.'[138] It's linked to an internal locus of control and shape of mind that says, 'I'm okay with you holding me to my word'.[139] High-performing teams have developed a level of accountability to themselves, to one another and to the purpose of the team or project.[140]

Of course, it's always easier to say 'we need accountability' than to ensure it's happening. Sticking to lots of small deadlines is at the very core of delivering projects on time. But we all know that sticking to deadlines and commitments (or being accountable) is hard whether the deadlines are small or not. It takes some personal maturity to develop the skill of not overcommitting (optimism bias affects us all) and staying on task when new shiny distractions arise. Frankly, it's part of being human to struggle with accountability.

Accountability gets a bad rap

Accountability is one of those words that often makes us feel uncomfortable. It has some poor associations with public humiliation and shaming. The version of accountability that operates from a place of humiliation to elicit compliance is not one that I have found personally motivating. It reminds me of the parent who loses their temper with their child and then berates the child with, 'If you hadn't done X, I wouldn't have lost my temper!' The child doesn't have the capacity to be accountable in that context and it leaves them confused and ashamed

138 Merriam-Webster. (n.d.). Accountability. https://www.merriam-webster.com/dictionary/accountability.

139 'Here it is: The real meaning of accountability in the workplace.' Range. https://www.range.co/blog/accountability-in-the-workplace.

140 Hall, J. (6 October 2019). 'Why Accountability Is Vital To Your Company.' *Forbes.* https://www.forbes.com/sites/johnhall/2019/10/06/why-accountability-is-vital-to-your-company/?sh=504893f56580.

or embarrassed. Sure, that feeling of 'I'll show them' can light a fire inside some, but operating from a place of fear and even hatred has a cost.

Coming instead from a place of aspiring to be better has been a healthier and more balanced choice for me. Thinking of accountability like a bridge that will move us closer to the aspirational version of ourselves is, to me, a way to frame accountability that makes it a more palatable topic.

The difference between accountability and shaming is one of placement of responsibility. Accountability is taking responsibility for your *actions* (or holding another person accountable for their actions). It's not about the individual. It's not about calling someone out in the hope they fix their mistakes – that can be taken as a personal attack. Shame is name calling. It's saying, 'You're a bad person'. But accountability is saying, 'You are expected to do this job' and then if the job is not done, finding out why and what can be done to get the job done.

> **The difference between accountability and shaming is one of placement of responsibility.**

So when we're considering the flavour of accountability that we're interested in developing with our own teams, we're aiming for a more compassionate accountability. I'm impressed by the work of Jane Dutton and Monica Worlain who focus on bringing compassion to organisations. They have found in their research that compassion not only leads to better accountability, but can also be a competitive advantage, leading to benefits in areas like innovation, collaboration, service quality and even talent retention.[141]

---

141 Worline, M & Dutton, J. (2018). *Awakening Compassion At Work: The Quiet Power That Elevates People and Organizations*. Berrett-Koehler.

Precondition for compassionate accountability

To be able to hold myself or others to account in a compassionate way, there must first be a precondition of care. Fundamentally, that means that we care about the work we're doing or are about to do. It means that anyone taking on the work is thinking, 'I want to do it well.' But to have compassionate accountability within a project the entire team and organisation must also be focused on doing it well. That means that we're functioning within a culture where doing something well is important and valued. There's no point in bringing standards to a place where standards don't matter.

Again, I think here of my son's new job at a place where standards really matter. From his first day on the job, it was made abundantly clear to him that he was part of a team that was responsible for public safety and that not taking that seriously could and would have serious and real consequences. And that means that he's known those standards from the outset and has felt the keen responsibility of ensuring they're met both individually and as part of his team.

His company cares. His team cares. And now my son cares. And that is the very first step in real accountability.

Extreme accountability & the 4 laws that underpin it

Accountability is an incredibly difficult thing to do alone. We can try to rely on our own discipline and willpower, but our own desire to 'do well' is just not enough. An easier path is to build systems around us that make it the default to do the aspirational thing.

David Goggins, a retired Navy SEAL and ultra-endurance athlete, has conceptualised extreme accountability work which has seen him going from poverty and abuse to one of the toughest men alive. The core of his idea is adopting the 'can't hurt me' mindset and pushing past your own self-imposed limitations and discomfort. But another requirement is to take what he calls extreme ownership of one's own life. Goggins holds himself fully accountable for his past mistakes, his poor choices and his actions and decisions, and believes that this is the only path to real self-improvement.[142]

James Clear has a model that he recommends for creating behaviour change. He calls them the four laws.

1. Focus on making the aspirational behaviour **obvious** (place it on a path where you will not miss it).

2. Focus on making it **attractive** (something you want to do).

3. Focus on making it **easy** (taking a smaller step).

4. And focus on making it **satisfying** (getting a reward).[143]

These four laws apply well to our goal of building accountability in change projects. Spending some effort in setting up systems that help us do the aspirational things more easily and building in some level of reward for doing so is a good way to get ourselves comfortable with staying accountable.

---

142 Goggins, D. (2018). *Can't Hurt Me: Master Your Mind and Defy the Odds*. Lioncrest Publishing.
143 Clear. Atomic Habits.

Personal accountability – accountability starts with me

In my early thirties I received a diagnosis that shifted my relationship to my own health.

I can clearly recall the moment. I'm sitting next to a nurse at a computer screen. In the very matter of fact way that nurses are infamous for, she shares my diagnosis and follows up with the news that I'll be on medication for the rest of my life. Pinpricks of 'sorry for myself' tears are poised on the threshold of becoming full blown sobs.

The rest of my life? If I live to 80 that's close to 50 years!

She probably delivers this type of news all the time so she reassures me with 'it could be worse'. But I'm too young and healthy to take pills every day – that's what sick people do.

So, I resolve at 'some point' (not today, but someday) things will get better – this will not be my forever fate. The immediate reality is that I must take the medication, follow the instructions and regain my strength. I am a rule follower (most of the time) so I do all the things that I'm instructed by the doctors.

But in the background, I'm researching and figuring out other ways to manage my condition. Ayurvedic medicine, broadly based on the belief that each person is responsible for their own health and wellbeing and that you are the best doctor for you, becomes part of the research process and I go to other doctors. I make changes to my diet, my stress management, my relationship to work and I add Ayurvedic supplements. Through this process my relationship to my own health shifts.

I become accountable for making decisions for my health. I feel more responsible for my own health than I previously did. It's both reassuring and terrifying.

Personal accountability is the first step in creating accountability within a change project. And leaders play an important part of emulating that. In fact, sometimes just one conversation – one request for accountability – can have a lasting impact on a person. I'm reminded of the situation where I had quite a difficult conversation with somebody who was very emotional about their situation. As we chatted I invited them to consider what it was that they were able to own themselves and act on in this situation. They took that on board, we talked some more and then they went on their way. I didn't believe that what I'd said would have any real impact, or that they'd make any real change. Most people don't, after all.

About a year later when the person was leaving the business, they came by to thank me for having shown belief in them. Even though, at the time, I thought that I'd missed the mark and that nothing would change, it did. When leaders create the opportunity for others to believe in themselves and see themselves in a different way, it's an enormous service to them. And if you aren't delivering those opportunities for accountability to your team (if accountability *doesn't* start with 'me'), then you're letting them down. If accountability starts with me, then it needs to be woven into the very fabric of our working life – both personally and organisationally.

Tactics for improving personal accountability

I am a chronic conflict avoider. I have a theory that the thing that makes me encourage and create accountability may just be that it's a pathway to avoid conflict. I'm looking to develop self-managing systems that will reinforce the aspirational behaviors and push me in the right direction without having an argument about it (even an internal debate).

Despite my accountability/conflict theory, in reality, there aren't many people who actively want to be held accountable (by themselves or by someone else). But it's one of those things that we all have to face up to at some point if we want to lift standards and improve the game. It's a little bit like my health diagnosis. At some point in your life, you need to take charge of your accountability or be a victim of it (and for me, face more unwanted conflict).

Here are some tactics that I've used over the years as a serving suggestion for those who are keen to improve personal accountability to a plan.

1. **Write it down.** I try to remember to make a daily action plan and a weekly action plan so that I'm clear about what it is that I want to get done for the week. When I find myself wandering, I come back to this list and refocus. This is not an 'always done' type of thing, but when I do it, I'm way more on top of things and much more focused on what I really need to do. It creates clarity within my own practice and mind.

2. **Make space.** Once I've figured out the list, I then put this into the schedule, allocating actual time in my calendar to do the tasks in the action plan. Typically, my estimates are wildly off when it comes to how long it takes to do something, especially when it's my first time with a specific task. So I'll often have to move things around to make up for those inaccuracies, but because it's on the calendar then even if it gets moved or bumped, I just find another spot for it. The result is that I end up making space for it at some point or another, and it keeps me accountable to myself.

3. **Set reminders.** I set reminders for myself during the day. My children laugh at me about how many reminders and timers I have. When I've got a big block of time that isn't scheduled,

I break it down into smaller blocks of time so that I don't get distracted and just end up trolling the internet for four or five hours.

4. **Have time without emails and notifications.** This has been a really big shift for me. Not having email, Slack, Messenger and Teams open all the time gives me some focused, uninterrupted time to get tasks completed. It really reduces my capacity to get distracted. This one simple change has made me a lot more productive in the way that I'm working, and I feel less 'on edge'. And it allows me to be more accountable.

Group accountability – decide what's okay and what's not

When we work on accountability behaviours in teams, we start by looking to articulate what's okay and what's not okay[144] – to share a set of behaviours and guidelines that explain how we will and won't work together. This is our foundation for building group accountability, because without this framework, we don't have any benchmarks for accountability.

According to the research, when people feel seen, supported and empowered, they do their best work.[145] Holding your people accountable in a group setting can do all of these things, particularly in an organisation where they feel that accountability is being done with some compassion. In that case, it's much more likely that the team will feel inspired to invest *more* in the organisation to reach the aspirational

---

144 (2024). Dare to Lead: The BRAVING Inventory. Brené Brown. https://brenebrown. com/resources/the-braving-inventory/.

145 Worline. Awakening Compassion At Work.

goals set, rather than shrink back away from tasks that would require their accountability.

Insight into group behaviour

If you're trying to improve accountability in a team here are some things to consider around group behaviour that can help:

1. When we treat a group just as 'a cohesive singular group' rather than a set of individuals, then everyone thinks 'someone else will do that'. But when everyone thinks that someone else will do it, then no one does in the end. Onlookers remain silent because they think that in a group, they don't make much of a difference. This is a lesson I've learned the hard way. You can't have an action item and no owner for it. Even if the whole group needs to contribute, someone needs to take responsibility for each task.

2. Just because onlookers are silent in the group or in the moment doesn't mean that they're not paying attention. They're taking careful notes about consistency and the behaviour of leaders. Whether you hear about it in the meeting, or it happens in the hallways post, consistency is being noted, compared and critiqued.

3. Every 'free pass' adds up. Dan Ariely, an American psychology and behavioural economics professor at Duke, sums up our human tendency to let ourselves off the hook with the phrase 'everyone cheats a little from time to time'.[146] His experiments reveal that when we have a 'free pass' to cheat, the results are remarkably consistent – lots of people cheat a little. He

---

146 Grant, A. (31 March 2014). Dan Aierly on 'The Honest Truth About Dishonesty'. Knowledge at Wharton. Wharton School of the University of Pennsylvania. https://knowledge.wharton.upenn.edu/article/dan-ariely-dishonestys-slippery-slope/.

calls this a 'personal fudge factor' that we allow ourselves.[147] In the same way, if we give ourselves a free pass to not deliver something that a team member is waiting on, then progress slows and frustration increases. Clarity about when something is needed and what the next steps are help each person to better understand the context and dependencies of their work. When there's a dependency, encourage the people involved to work out how the work will be handed off.

4. Holding other people to account can be a difficult business. Some research shows that it improves the performance of a team when there are no freeloaders.[148] So in that way, having a person who keeps everyone accountable is a great thing. The problem is that often the person who steps up to do the work of holding others to account suffers for it. Their likeability in the group is compromised and their interpersonal discomfort increases. While getting used to interpersonal discomfort is something that gets easier the more you practice it, that doesn't make it a nice job. Rather than foisting this responsibility onto a single person, sometimes a framework for feedback is required so that people can gain insight into what's not working and what's needed to shift that without relying on just a single person.

These group behaviours are just that – behaviours that tend to occur in groups. None of this is intended to demean anyone. It's just an acknowledgement that we're all human and fallible and that in the pursuit of something 'better' than the current situation we will very likely

---

147 Ted. (19 March 2009). Why we think it's OK to cheat and steal (sometimes). Dan Ariely [Video]. YouTube. https://www.youtube.com/watch?v=nUdsTizSxSl.

148 Overfield, D & Kaiser, R. (8 November 2012). 'One Out of Every Two Managers Is Terrible at Accountability,' *Harvard Business Review*. https://hbr.org/2012/11/one-out-of-every-two-managers-is-terrible-at-accountability.

fall short of our own aspirations. And the more we know about group dynamics, the better we'll be able to operate within them.

How do we foster accountability in project teams?

The number one way that we create accountability to the project team is through connection and compassion. This starts with leaders modelling accountable behaviour and openly discussing both successes and failures. People who feel more personally connected are more committed to the group and the outcomes we're striving for.

When it comes to accountability in the project team, encourage team members to hold each other accountable, and not just wait for top-down enforcement. Having an external party (like a project manager) hold the space for the project team to live up to the commitments and promises of the project, can also shift the group dynamic. An external person is less sensitive to internal politics and the interpersonal discomfort that can be felt by someone holding themselves and the team to account.

Tips to foster accountability in project teams:

1. **Define what's expected and how we will work.** I very much like the way Brené Brown states this in very simple 'what's okay / not okay' statements.[149] Clarity of the goals, the scope and the ways we will work all help to foster good working methods and keep us on track with the interdependent work we have in projects.

2. **Keep your eye on the purpose.** Reminding ourselves who is relying on us and how that will impact the rest of the project helps to keep the 'free pass' tendency under control. It can also

---

149 Brown. Dare to Lead.

work to have a project 'buddy' to keep you on track. We often use action lists and review them regularly with our project team members. Remember it's a continuing evolution. There's no one perfect way to do this. Each project and group of people has its own characteristics.

3. **Take consistent, small steps.** Small, buy-in actions can have a big impact when it comes to cultivating compassion and accountability. This makes it easier to stick to deadlines and commitments and gives each person ongoing wins under their belts which further incentivises them to stay accountable going forward.

4. **Compliment and acknowledge when things go well.** It's easy to offer encouragement and support when things are going to plan, but it's equally important to offer them when things are *not* going to plan. Sometimes discomfort is motivating. Project managers don't need to personally rescue people all the time and the discomfort of consequences that have arisen because you haven't done your part is a motivating lesson too.

How to build a culture of accountability

To quote Brené Brown:

> *'Setting boundaries and holding people accountable*
> *is a lot more work than shaming and blaming.*
> *But it's also much more effective.'*[150]

So, if you're keen to improve accountability effectiveness then know that accountability isn't a one-time event. It takes follow up and consistency. We've all had the moment when you've had to do something difficult that you don't want to do. Holding someone else to account is just as

---

150   Brown, B. (2010). *The Gifts of Imperfection.* Random House.

difficult. It feels awkward and confronting (especially when I know I'm guilty of messing up too). But there are ways to do it that are kind and compassionate, and that focuses on the *action* rather than the *individual*.

Here are a few suggestions that may be helpful as you embark on building a culture of accountability for your project.

1. Set clear expectations.

Before you can hold someone accountable, ensure that expectations are crystal clear. Using the SMART framework never hurts (specific, measurable, achievable, relevant and time-bound).[151] Alternatively building out the 'what's okay / not okay' framework can help you to better articulate expectations when it comes to boundaries and behaviour.[152]

Clearly defining what behaviours and outcomes are acceptable and which are not paints a more vivid picture of expectations. The 'what's okay / not okay' part addresses misinterpretations and extremes.

2. Address issues promptly and in private.

Prompt feedback prevents small problems from snowballing into larger ones. It can also keep things more low key because the sooner you tackle an issue, the less time it has to gather momentum and turn into something that gets out of control.

When it comes to addressing concerns, we also try to follow the rule of praise in public and feedback in private. There are some theories that suggest that all feedback might be more effective in promoting intrinsic

---

151 Ogbeiwi, O. (2017). 'Why written objectives need to be really SMART.'
     British Journal of Healthcare Management. https://www.researchgate.net/
     publication/318390296_Why_written_objectives_need_to_be_really_SMART.
152 Davis, G. (30 April 2017). FOR ACC Boundaries, Empathy, and Compassion [Video].
     YouTube. https://www.youtube.com/watch?v=xATF5uYVRkM&t=1s.

motivation when delivered privately.[153] But certainly there are many who find public criticism and even praise awkward and would rather be acknowledged one on one. This might be just a matter of catching someone after a meeting or spending 10 minutes getting some time together. Knowing your team and who you are working with and their preferred 'love language' for feedback is helpful here.

3. Use open ended questions.

Brené Brown has a list of what she calls 'rumble starters'[154] that can be used to initiate difficult conversations. These include things like, 'the story I make up', 'I'm curious about' and 'tell me more'. As I read through her list, I realise that I've got a version of many of these. I'm a particular fan of 'that's not my experience' – it doesn't deny another's experience whilst at the same time making the point that they may not have the only experience possible.

The reality is, no matter how much we might believe someone to be doing the 'wrong thing', in most cases, people are acting logically from their own point of view.[155] Trying to get a greater understanding of their point of view is an essential part of creating compassionate accountability and open-ended questions can help you get that understanding by setting the tone for an open, honest dialogue.

A good example of an open-ended question in context is, 'I'd like to discuss the project timeline. Can you walk me through your perspective

153 Fong, C, Patall, E, Vasquez, A & Stautberg, S. (15 August 2018). 'A Meta-Analysis of Negative Feedback on Intrinsic Motivation.' Educational Psychology Review. https://selfdeterminationtheory.org/wp-content/uploads/2019/11/2019_FongPatallETAL_EdPsychReview.pdf.

154 Brown, B. (1 May 2019). 'Let's Rumble.' Brené Brown. https://brenebrown.com/articles/2019/05/01/lets-rumble/.

155 Brown, B. (27 March 2020). 'Brené Brown on Comparative Suffering, the 50/50 Myth, and Settling the Ball.' Brené Brown. https://brenebrown.com/podcast/brene-on-comparative-suffering-the-50-50-myth-and-settling-the-ball/.

on why we're behind schedule?' This will help you to get to the root of not only the problem that you're confronting but what lies behind it as well.

4. Use project record keeping systems.

After any accountability discussions, document what was said, and any agreements made. This creates a record for future reference and ensures everyone is on the same page. (It's a way to stay 'accountable' about your 'accountability' discussion!) These records are also helpful by creating a future checkpoint where you can revisit commitments and track progress.

> As you check back in on your progress, continue to adjust your benchmarks – accountability isn't a one-time event.

As you check back in on your progress, continue to adjust your benchmarks – accountability isn't a one-time event. Following up regularly on progress and commitments is the job of the project manager but should also be supported by sponsors, stakeholders and line managers.

Sometimes, despite your best efforts, you'll need to have difficult conversations about persistent accountability issues. Make sure that you prepare for these conversations (write notes if you need to), remain calm and be clear about the consequences if improvements aren't made.

5. Lead by example.

As a leader or team member, model the accountability you expect from others. This means being transparent about your own goals, admitting when you make mistakes and taking responsibility for your actions. Balance this by recognising and celebrating when team members demonstrate strong accountability. Reinforcing positive behaviours is so much more fun than having to discipline and clean up after negative ones. And you'll get much better results as well.

Building accountable vendor relationships

Just like in all other parts of your change project, you need accountability with and between your vendors as part of your extended team. They are relying on you for critical business information delivered in a timely manner. And you need them to meet their responsibilities in bringing the technical skills and knowledge of your new system to the table by the deadlines you've discussed.

To ensure that you're supporting accountable vendor relationships you'll need to structure your communications and track requirements throughout the life of the project. And that means constructing your vendor agreements to build in chicken doors and checkpoints.

Chicken doors and checkpoints

What's a chicken door? It's something that I first encountered on a family holiday to Disneyland as a teenager.[156] The experience of being in Disneyland was incredibly exciting. The most daring ride at the time was Space Mountain. But I'm naturally a bit of a scaredy cat. If you know me, you know I'm not into roller coasters, scary movies or standing too close to the edge. I was the person who, at sleepovers, had my hands over my eyes when it came to watching horror movies, and I am always

---

156 Disneyland was just the first four days of a nine-week round the world trip that I still marvel at my parents for taking four children on.

the one who startles at the jump scare. It just seems like stress that I would rather not have, thank you very much.

The clever heads at Disney understood the psychology of people like me who get excited about the idea of doing the daring thing and then get to the actual top of the ride, have a real good look and realise, 'maybe this isn't for me'. So, they had—I'm not sure if it still exists—what was colloquially referred to as the chicken door. It's an escape door that allows you to opt out as you get close to the top of the queue.

Once you got to a point where we could see some of the ride, there was the option to leave if it wasn't really for you. However, once you've gone past the chicken door, you're committed, and you were definitely going ahead with the ride. There's no way out. You better believe I used that chicken door once I saw the speed of the take off, the flashing lights and the dark tunnel that marked the entrance of Space Mountain!

It's worth having the chicken door kind of mindset when it comes to constructing vendor agreements and building relationships. Heading into large software projects can be the kind of thing that seems like a great idea when you first join the queue but could pale the closer you get to the reality of what's happening. In this case, you might choose to do a proof-of-concept before committing to the full effort. This gives you a way to evaluate whether an idea works while still having some control over the risk. By building in checks as the project work progresses you can ensure that what you're being told is there, true and really working to the extent that you've been sold.

Checkpoints to create accountable vendor relationships

You've heard the phrase 'trust but verify'? When you're setting up your vendor agreements, this is the time to live by that phrase. Each verification point is essentially a checkpoint. So, how does this work?

1. Establish vendor touchpoints

The larger the project and business, the more internal touch points the vendor should have with you. There should be a working level day-to-day, getting stuff done kind of relationship with touchpoints to match. We would also expect to see a project level relationship (with your project manager and the vendor's project manager), then maybe an account level relationship and then an executive level relationship.

All these people should be familiar enough with each other to respond quickly and to be able to connect one on one when needed without the requirement for multiple parties to get involved. It gives you a clear path for escalation if the project efforts are not going as planned. Inside your business, there should be more than one executive who's across the project and intimate enough with the details of the work.

This all needs to be built into your relationships, but also into your vendor agreements, to ensure the touchpoints (checkpoints) are clear for everyone involved.

2. Include cross checks

You also need to add review points and clear delivery gateways in your agreements, as well as your project plan. Ensure that contract provisions and penalties are both general and specific enough to drive the behaviour that you're looking for.

One way to do this is to have the software vendor (if possible) check, validate or guarantee the work of the system implementation partner. Or to create points sometimes referred to as 'gateways' where there are standards and targets must be achieved for the project to progress to the next stage. It's a way of building control points.

One of the best ways I've seen this done is by an agency that was given a review by the people who built some new software. The agency working on it had a code review which the client paid for. It was to ensure that the code that was being developed was optimised in the best possible way and that any future technical debt was called out. It also ensured that the client understood what they were getting. The process of having the software vendor check the system implementation partners work (to ensure that performance was up to expectations) meant that anything that wasn't working well would be caught and brought up to meet the client's needs.

3. Use mutual embedding

One super practical thing you can do (as old school as it sounds) is to consider mutual embedding with the vendor across your team. This might mean that a couple of people from your team go to work with the vendor from time to time. And, likewise, some of the vendor's people will come to work with you.

Of course, this is not always feasible, particularly in global relationships. But where it is possible, it really helps to build an understanding of how both businesses work, and it allows the development of much stronger working relationships.

Embedding, if managed well, can also increase decision-making speed during essential points in the change project process where otherwise decisions might be drawn out. Setting a few days aside to get all the right people in a room and get the design signed off can save weeks of back and forth via email to gain sign offs.

Accountability reinforces commitment

Accountability ensures that commitments within your change project are met. But it's not just about creating personal accountability, accountability within our teams and accountability with our vendors and partners. It's about building the framework where that accountability can thrive. And a huge part of that is your communication – because it's the quality of your communication that reinforces those commitments.

Kind Communication

Politeness and good manners were expected when I was growing up. Not talking back to adults and showing that you were listening when they spoke was a part of this. It took me well into my teen years to understand my Irish grandfather. His accent was broad (and it got broader the longer the party went on). But I still nodded politely. I was well behaved, and it would never have occurred to me to do more than politely smile and nod and hope that this was an appropriate response to whatever he was saying.

In the nuanced terrain of human interaction, particularly within project teams, the distinction between politeness and kindness emerges both in intent and impact. Politeness often operates as a social lubricant. Just like my smiles and nods to my grandfather, when we're being polite, we're not deeply engaged. Instead, we're adhering to social norms and expectations to create smooth interactions (sometimes in the hope that it will be over soon). When we're working in global teams it's of particular significance to bring some understanding of what is considered polite in other cultures, both not to offend or be offended.

Politeness versus kindness

I often think of politeness as what my nana would have called 'manners' – that is courteous and professional. These matter in our personal lives, of course. But while politeness and manners can help maintain a harmonious working environment, it's kindness that builds deeper levels of trust and respect in a team.

That's because kindness is motivated by a genuine concern for others. It goes beyond the surface level of pleasant interactions, aiming to positively impact someone's life, even if it requires uncomfortable truths or actions that are not immediately rewarding. The intent behind kindness is not just to be viewed as nice but to foster a real, positive change in others' lives. This can be particularly impactful in project teams where collaboration and mutual support are key to success. When team members are kind, they are more likely to go the extra mile for each other, offer support during difficult moments and provide constructive feedback that contributes to personal and professional growth and the achievement of shared goals.

Research underscores that engaging in acts of kindness not only boosts the mental health of the recipient[157] but also that of the giver, reducing stress and enhancing emotional well-being.[158] In the context of project teams, the power of kindness can be transformative. For instance,

---

157　(17 February 2023). 'The Mental Health Benefits of Simple Acts of Kindness.' American Psychiatric Association. https://www.psychiatry.org/news-room/apa-blogs/mental-health-benefits-simple-acts-of-kindness.

158　Post S. (2014). 'It's Good To Be Good: 2014 Biennial Scientific Report on Health, Happiness, Longevity, and Helping Others.' *International Journal of Person Centered Medicine.* https://unlimitedloveinstitute.org/downloads/ITS-GOOD-TO-BE-GOOD-2014-Biennial-Scientific-Report-On-Health-Happiness-Longevity-And-Helping-Others.pdf.

simple acts like giving meaningful compliments, can significantly boost team morale.[159]

Adam Grant, Professor at Wharton specialising in organisational change agrees.

> *'Politeness is not the same as kindness. Being polite is saying what makes people feel good today. Being kind is doing what helps people get better tomorrow.*
>
> *In polite cultures, people withhold disagreement and criticism. In kind cultures, people speak their minds respectfully.'*

Kindness doesn't mean reticence

We can still be kind and speak our mind. Developing confidence in challenging one another (a kindness) that will allow us to improve how we lift performance across the whole business will be a part of how we work with the end-to-end processes.

Workplace cultures that prioritise acts of kindness, often report higher levels of employee satisfaction and lower turnover rates.[160] Demonstrating kindness through transparent communication, showing genuine interest in teammates' well-being and practicing empathy can foster a sense of belonging and acceptance.

If you're in need of some suggestions for creating greater kindness in your team, consider these.

---

159 Boothby, E, Zhao, X & Bohns, V. (24 February 2021). 'A Simple Compliment Can Make a Big Difference.' *Harvard Business Review.* https://hbr.org/2021/02/a-simple-compliment-can-make-a-big-difference.

160 Swinalang, A. (21 July 2023). 'Why Kindness at Work Pays Off.' *Harvard Business Review.* https://hbr.org/2023/07/why-kindness-at-work-pays-off.

- **Pay it forward** — treat a colleague by bringing them a coffee or offering assistance on a task they're working on.

- **Express gratitude** — send a thank-you email or note to a team member who has gone above and beyond or has been particularly supportive.

- **Smile or greet your team** — a simple smile or greeting can create a positive atmosphere and build a sense of camaraderie.

- **Acknowledge great work** — compliment a colleague on a job well done, whether it's during a meeting or in a personal conversation. Let them know their efforts are appreciated.

The other thing that I try to do is find something awesome about every person that I interact with on the client team and make a note of that awesome trait. It's a great way to create meaningful ways to remember names too!

Candid

Kind communication is candid communication. It's honest communication. Patty McCord, author of *Powerful* and a founding contributor to the legendary culture at Netflix (you know, the slide deck that has been viewed more than 16 million times[161]), recounts in her book the path that Netflix took to stripping away bureaucracy and developing strong disciplines in their culture.[162] They developed an environment that encouraged 'open, clear and constant communication, the practice of radical honesty that was timely and face to face, strong fact-based opinions and rigour around debate.'[163]

---

161 Archived version available at: Callahan, E. 'Netflix Culture Deck.' Entrepreneurial Operating System. https://www.eosworldwide.com/blog/103242-eos-netflix-culture-deck.

162 McCord, P. (2018). *Powerful: Building a Culture of Freedom and Responsibility.* Silicon Guild.

163 McCord. Powerful.

The radical honesty of the culture that carried Netflix through an extraordinary period of growth and innovation is not necessarily right for everyone. The culture might not be one to emulate but the dedication the Netflix team gave to their cultural code was legendary and a significant contributing factor to the success of the business as it evolved. The real lesson to take away here is the benefit of encoding accountability into the culture of your business and including that in how we work and communicate with each other. This is a lesson that I think has some merit in being applied to other environments.

The Netflix focus was to take away as many layers as possible in terms of procedures and policies and to elevate the transparency and honesty they'd already built to continue to ensure that people understood the right thing to do. How we name it is not the most important part. Call it civility, or radical candour or a manifesto. The most important part is that the people part of the plan gets attention. And that we revisit it, frequently.

Why adaptability matters in honest communication

The business of your business (of any business) is evolving all the time, and your teams need to evolve as well. This is not just to meet the needs of the business but also to meet the aspirations of the people that make up the business. In our project work, we work with teams who are at varying stages of development and evolution. Teams who are just starting out need vision and alignment of purpose according to HBR[164] and as teams grow, leaders need to adapt their style.[165]

---

164 de Mol, E. (21 March 2019). 'What Makes a Successful Startup Team.' *Harvard Business Review.* https://hbr.org/2019/03/what-makes-a-successful-startup-team.
165 Zhuo, J. (13 March 2019). 'As Your Team Gets Bigger, Your Leadership Style Has to Adapt.' *Harvard Business Review.* https://hbr.org/2019/03/as-your-team-gets-bigger-your-leadership-style-has-to-adapt.

Making sure that as your project comes to life you've considered how the people plan and the communication around that people plan will evolve is a critical part of your success. Communication processes that drove honesty and openness in the beginning of a project may no longer do so as things progress and change. We have seen exciting businesses with vision and ideas, with financial workability and operational expertise, fall because they haven't thought through how to create a flexible and adaptable system of communications or implemented a decision-making framework that will allow them to move quickly when things change.

> **Making sure that as your project comes to life you've considered how the people plan and the communication around that people plan will evolve is a critical part of your success.**

Kindness is taking responsibility

When it comes to communication in a project environment, the kindest thing that we can do is to take responsibility for our own part in the communication. If you look at a textbook version of communication explained, it's shown as a send, transmit and receive linear type of model.

But in reality true communication is not just send, transmit and receive. It's so many other pieces: the creation of the idea and message, the processing, the context of the receiver, the (sometimes) visceral reaction to the message, the checking and the understanding of the message. And in all that mess, it's very easy to see how messages get mixed up and misinterpreted.

When we are inexact with our expression, it's easy for our intended message to get lost. Hannah Gadsby, Australian comedian talks about her mother's ability to tell the story, and *always* land the story plane … even if it's on your face.[166] We need to think about our communications in the same way. Even if you've been exact, that doesn't guarantee the safe landing of the 'message plane'. The crafting of messages for large groups of people takes effort, thought and many drafts. Speechwriters, copywriters, graphic designers and HR teams, all obsess over the choice of words and the tone for just this reason.

Nonverbal communication

There are multitudes of ways that we communicate in the workplace, and we need to take responsibility for our part in each of them. And this includes how we show up physically. Posture, eye contact, how we dress, how we sit and move and how we interact with others – all of these things convey subtle messages to our colleagues about us. Some of this is conscious and trainable, and some of it is at a much lower level. Learning about nonverbal communication will help you to take responsibility for this element of your messaging.

Written communication

Increasingly, in project teams, we need to be able to communicate well in writing because a lot of the time we're working with international teams, and the lingua franca is increasingly English. So being clear, concise and to the point in communication is really important. When we are being concise, we're focused and accurate. When we're clear we avoid buzzwords and jargon and lead with the most important thing.

---

166 McGlynn, N. (18 May 2023). 'Hannah Gadsby: Something Special ~ The Jester's Privilege.' *Medium*. https://nickmcglynnjokes.medium.com/hannah-gadsby-something-special-the-jesters-privilege-89e90d441449.

In a written format, the use of headings, numbered lists, bolding and different coloured texts helps draw attention to the most important parts of the communication. Put the most important thing at the top of the list, and number it. Do the same thing when you're preparing for meetings – always put the most important agenda item, even if it's the most hairy agenda item, at the top. These things allow you to take responsibility for your part in the communication.

I think the other part of written communication (and taking responsibility for it) is taking a moment to consider how easy and complete it is for the receiver to digest. To assist with cutting through email traffic, work on giving subject lines with some kind of context marker that tells the recipient whether this is an FYI, a read and respond, a decision requested or a simple confirmation. If action is needed, then 'action required' is often the heading that I put in the email subject line. If the response is required by a certain time, adding that is also helpful. Is there an obvious, logical next question that the receiver will have?

One of the ways I have been able to help myself make sure that I'm sending a clear message is to read aloud to myself. This really only works in an environment where you've got the privacy to be able to do that. And I don't always have that. But when I can, it makes all the difference.

Closed loop communication

The other part is what I call closing the loop, which is helpful in small meetings or working sessions. This means summarising, repeating back and confirming any action or decision points that have been discussed.

When we're doing this by voice, it's pretty easy. You can ask the other person to just repeat back what it is that you think that you've done. You can ask, 'so what did you get out of that?' Or, 'can I just confirm what you've understood?' These sorts of open questions invite people to restate what it is that they're going away with in particular. And when it comes to an action meeting where you've had a discussion about what to do, and then you're agreeing on action, I think it's really helpful to have each person come back with, 'Okay, what am I doing? And by when?' Then it's very clear what the responsibility is.

Everyone cheats a little

Remember when we discussed how everyone cheats a little? Often, people say that they tell 'white lies' to protect somebody else's feelings. I know that when I'm telling a white lie, it's often because I don't want to have an awkward or uncomfortable conversation with somebody. Maybe I think they'll have a big reaction, and that will take a long time to get through. Maybe I'm protecting myself and trying to avoid discomfort. Whatever the reason, we all tell these little white lies where we want to avoid any form of confrontation or discomfort in our communication.

This was so well illustrated when I was having a conversation with a coach the other day, and she related a story about her children who had just been to a holiday tennis camp for intensive training. After the camp, the training coach had messaged her and asked, 'Do the kids want to come back for another one-on-one coaching session?' They did not. They had found the one-on-one very difficult. She acknowledged that she probably would've just fluffed this and said, 'Oh, they're busy today, or I don't think that's going to work. Or their aunt is visiting today.' All of those white lies that we perpetuate.

But her husband had the confidence and, I think, the kindness to say to the coach, 'I'm sorry. The kids found it really hard, so they're not really enthusiastic about coming back.' And what was interesting was what the coach did with that piece of information. He came back to the parents and said, 'They're right. It *was* hard. It was deliberately hard. I was pushing them. I was pushing them because I wanted to see how they would cope with the additional load. I was trying to make them better.' He then pointed out what the kids did well and praised them for sticking with it. Once the parents relayed that message, the kids were much more interested in going back and doing some more coaching.

This is a really great example of how being kind but truthful about what it is that you're feeling or what your experience is is a powerful way to allow for both the coach to adjust and evolve and also for the kids to adjust and evolve. And the problem with – 'I'm sorry, the schedule doesn't work' – is that no one gets better in that situation. Everyone just kind of goes to their corner and has whatever feelings they have about it having been too hard and not meeting expectations.

How honest (and kind) is your communication?

Adam Grant says that it's harder, but also kinder, to express opinions that make us better tomorrow. What's easy, and often the unspoken rule we all obey, is that we say something that makes everyone feel comfortable today rather than express the opinions that make us better tomorrow. As Ed Catmull puts it, if you have more candour in the hallways after the meeting than in the meetings themselves, then you have a problem.

The intersection of accountability and communication

This intersection of accountability and communication is critical to the success of any change project. These two things allow you to be clear with your team, with your vendors and with all your stakeholders, and ensure that everyone remains committed to their roles and aligned to the project's purpose. This relationship builds trust and cultivates a culture where reliability and high performance thrive.

Conclusion

The intent of this book is to share what I've learned over many years and through many different experiences in change projects in the hope that it will enable you to skip over some of the pitfalls that might otherwise pull you down.

While the very nature of this discussion means you'll be able to pull out some practical tips on how to select your vendor, bring your team together, work through the steps of project implementation and get your improvements into the operational sphere, this isn't the main thrust of this book. You won't have learned the benefits of scrum or kanban or be able to compare them against each other (maybe that will be the next book!).

What I have covered, instead, are the big picture structure, thoughts and mindset items that come into play when you're setting up and implementing your change project. These are the things that can substantially move your project along the path to success when done well... or undermine it (with potentially severe consequences!) when they aren't.

So what have we covered?

- **Understanding the context** – both micro and macro – that you're operating in, and the impact this could have on your project. And in the world that we're currently in, there are a lot of potential impacts to keep a vigilant look out for.

- **The duality of projects**, and how they sit outside the context of daily business needs and at the same time must serve the future strategy of the business. A tricky balance, but one that can be achieved with the right attention from sponsors and leadership teams.

- **The importance of purpose**. Project duality naturally leads to a discussion of finding and implementing your purpose. Operations keep the lights on – but projects are strategy. So, a project, at its very heart, must have a purpose that contributes to the long-term strategy of the business. Whether the project is divesting and closing a division, improving the use of technology or implementing a business-wide system, if it is not aligned with the strategic direction of the business, then the question must be asked: 'Why are we even considering this project?'

- Understanding your purpose helps you to take the next necessary step, and that's **adopting a customer-centric change strategy**. As we said, projects are the vehicles of possibility. They're born from strategic directives and they're what you need to close the gap between the actual (where you are) and the aspirational (where your purpose drives you to be).

- Part of closing this gap is **understanding alignment**. Gulati's book emphasises that purpose – or crafting a purpose – must go far beyond just being a poster on the wall.

- Capable leaders **embed a purpose and a vision in everything they do** – bringing their teams, their partners and their projects into alignment with that purpose and vision.

- **Transparency is the foundation** that supports collaboration and trust among team members, and allows them to work to their purpose in alignment. On the other hand, without it, even the most aligned and well-intentioned teams can falter.

- Of course, all of this means nothing if we can't **take action to implement our project**. And action usually comes in three phases: software selection, software implementation and the third and often forgotten phase, learning to use the full benefits of the software.

- Once your action stage is done, however, that's not the end. You will also need to have implemented accountability and kind communication that can see you reviewing and adjusting, reviewing and adjusting, to ultimately bring you through to the end of your project successfully.

A lot needs to go well (or reasonably well)

One of the most important things that I'd like you to take away from this book is that there are a lot of working parts that must go reasonably well (at least) for a project to reach success. You can think of this like a sports team.

In order to win the cup, the premiership, the flag or whatever competition you're in, many things have to go well. There must be solid preparation and planning around training, nutrition, sleep and fitness for the team. Coaches must be on point to get the best from the athletes. Management teams need to recruit and resource the right coaching and support staff, as well as have the funds to support athletes. The team must perform well on the day (or on many game days, depending on the competition).

Add to all of this a little bit of 'luck' in terms of circumstances going your way. Lack of significant injury, order of the draw (whether it's home or away), and how other teams perform are all outside any team's control but do play a part in how a season builds.

Just like a sports team, a project team is made up of many more people than those who are on the field (or taking action on the project). Focusing on one element will not build the whole team to deliver. What's needed is that attention be given to all the elements. Depending on the size of the business, board members, owners, sponsors and managers must all be behind the work that is at hand. Those at the action end need clarity on the vision and purpose of the project effort; this builds alignment towards the purpose of the project.

The business is not the same shape after – and it shouldn't be

Finally, the last message of this book is that implementation success lives beyond the life of the project. Remember that you have more than one summit to climb. In many cases, project success will live or die depending on how an organisation adjusts and accommodates the new piece of software and processes into their ongoing operations – or ascends to the second summit. Making transformation goals stick is a challenge that many businesses face.

Even when a business has successfully navigated an initial transformation, it's often struggling three years later. It's possible that some of the underlying reasons for this lapse are because strategy has changed or that the business has moved on, but that can't be everything. Lived experience gives a different lens to this. I've observed that often the project is a stretch for the organisation, and there's an underlying assumption that when complete, they're going to contract back to where they were in terms of operational support.

In fact, when the project is a stretch, it gives the organisation a slightly different shape on the other side. And that's a good thing.

It's a bit like getting a new car. If you upgrade from a 20-year-old Corolla to a brand new Range Rover, then the maintenance and insurance costs are going to change. The street parking that was fine for the old car might not be where you want to leave the new one. The new car may need additional attention and services in the first months of ownership. Things that support those two cars are going to be quite different. And how you use the car might change as well.

In the same way, leaders in a business post change need to consider what the structure of the business teams will look like after software implementation is complete and who will own the ongoing improvements and maintenance of this new tool. Thinking and planning ahead of time about how the new system will be housed and maintained is a critical step that often business sponsors miss prior to starting the project.

In the end, it's the operational teams who must take ownership of the new systems and the changed processes and methods that have evolved through the project. They must adapt to their new ways of working as the business grows and evolves. If the business team doesn't act and changes are not embedded with owners, then things go from being a lovely new ride to a badly maintained mess over time.

Being prepared for the second summit, and for the changed state of your business, is vital to your ongoing success – and I hope this book has helped set you on the road to getting the most out of your change project.

Work with Leonie

In today's rapidly evolving retail landscape, the need for expert guidance to navigate complex technological changes is more critical than ever. Leonie brings over 20 years of experience in supporting customer-centric organisations in the retail sector, particularly in implementing and optimising systems and technology solutions such as ERP, PLM, PIM, e-commerce, MarTech, middleware and warehouse systems.

Leonie is renowned for her ability to lead complex technology transformation projects, consistently aligning IT providers with the specific needs of her clients. Her approach is grounded in building positive and collaborative relationships among stakeholders and challenging the status quo with a practical Land direct perspective.

As a leader, Leonie is committed to developing the potential of those she works with, creating new possibilities and opportunities for her clients.

Whether you're looking to lead a successful transformation project or navigate the challenges of technological change, Leonie's expertise and strategic insights can help you achieve your goals.

Leonie has partnered with a diverse range of prominent brands in the retail sector, from The Athlete's Foot to Baby Bunting.

Book a time to chat with Leonie here: https://bit.ly/3wYRLh6, or connect with her team at contact@6r.com.au.

Alternatively, visit Leonie's website at https://6r.com.au/ to learn more about her Retail Project Management Services, including Software Selection, Software Process Implementation, Mastering the Systems, as well as her workshops, coaching programs, and VIP days.

9 781763 761902